THE "I LOVE MY AIR FRYER"

Gluten-Free

RECIPE BOOK

From *Lemon Blueberry Muffins* to *Mediterranean Short Ribs*,
175 Easy and Delicious Gluten-Free Recipes

Michelle Fagone of CavegirlCuisine.com
Author of *The "I Love My Instant Pot®"
Gluten-Free Recipe Book*

Adams Media
New York   London   Toronto   Sydney   New Delhi

To Sam
Cheers to us and the crazy life we've created.
All my heart, M

Adams Media
An Imprint of Simon & Schuster, Inc.
100 Technology Center Drive
Stoughton, Massachusetts 02072

First Adams Media trade paperback edition June 2019

ADAMS MEDIA and colophon are trademarks of Simon & Schuster.

For information about special discounts for bulk purchases, please contact Simon & Schuster Special Sales at 1-866-506-1949 or business@simonandschuster.com.

The Simon & Schuster Speakers Bureau can bring authors to your live event. For more information or to book an event contact the Simon & Schuster Speakers Bureau at 1-866-248-3049 or visit our website at www.simonspeakers.com.

Photographs by James Stefiuk

Manufactured in China

10 9 8 7 6 5

Library of Congress Cataloging-in-Publication Data
Names: Fagone, Michelle, author.
Title: The "I love my air fryer" gluten-free recipe book / Michelle Fagone of CavegirlCuisine.com, author of The "I love my Instant Pot®" gluten-free recipe book.
Description: Avon, Massachusetts: Adams Media, 2019.
Series: "I love my" series.
Includes index.
Identifiers: LCCN 2019001246 | ISBN 9781507210413 (pb) | ISBN 9781507210420 (ebook)
Subjects: LCSH: Gluten-free diet--Recipes. | Hot air frying. | LCGFT: Cookbooks.
Classification: LCC RM237.86 .F339 2019 | DDC 641.5/639311--dc23
LC record available at https://lccn.loc.gov/2019001246

ISBN 978-1-5072-1041-3
ISBN 978-1-5072-1042-0 (ebook)

Contains material adapted from the following title published by Adams Media, an Imprint of Simon & Schuster, Inc.: The Everything® Air Fryer Cookbook by Michelle Fagone, copyright © 2018, ISBN 978-1-5072-0912-7.

Contents

Introduction

If you have an air fryer at home, you already know that it is a revolutionary appliance that can save you time and improve your health. New to this wonderful device? Well, you'll be excited to learn that you'll soon be using your air fryer to prepare everything from breakfast to dessert. But what's so special about air frying?

The air fryer can replace your oven, microwave, deep fryer, and dehydrator *and* cook delicious meals in a fraction of the time you're used to. If you're looking to provide your family with healthy meals, but don't have a lot of time to spare, the air fryer is a game changer!

The air fryer can also help with your success on a gluten-free diet. Typically, frying involves lots of oil and gluten-filled breading. However, in air frying, you still get that delicious crunch of fried food without the added grease, and you can choose your very own gluten-free breading. Another benefit to using the air fryer in a gluten-free lifestyle is the short cooking times it provides. Long-term success on a gluten-free diet is often attributed to ease of preparing healthy meals. That's why your air fryer will be your best friend throughout your gluten-free journey and help you stay on track, even on the days when you are short on time.

In *The "I Love My Air Fryer" Gluten-Free Recipe Book*, you'll learn everything you need to know about using an air fryer, as well as some basics that will help you find success while living a gluten-free lifestyle. You'll also discover the perfect recipe for any occasion, from satisfying breakfasts, like Loaded Breakfast Quesadillas, to delicious dinners for the whole family, such as Spaghetti Pie—and everything in between. So, let's get air frying!

Air Fryer Essentials

The air fryer has become a favorite kitchen appliance for good reason: fried foods can be made and eaten guilt-free! It can also cook foods quicker than the conventional oven, doesn't heat up your living space (which you'll be thankful for on those warm-weather days), and is easy to clean. In this chapter, you will learn more about the functions of the air fryer, its helpful accessories, and the benefits of air frying. You will also discover further information on the gluten-free diet, including how it can benefit your life.

Keep in mind that while this chapter will cover the basics of using your air fryer, the first step is reading the manual that came with your air fryer. All air fryers are different, and with the recent rise in popularity of the appliance there are a lot of different models on the market. Learning how to use your specific air fryer thoroughly is the key to success and will familiarize you with troubleshooting issues as well as safety functions. Reading over the manual and washing all parts with warm, soapy water before first use will help you feel ready to unleash your culinary finesse!

Why Air Frying?

So, who benefits from owning an air fryer? The answer is everyone! The air fryer works by baking foods with a constant stream of circulating hot air that cooks food evenly and quickly, crisping up edges as it does its job. This is why the air fryer has quicker cooking times than a conventional oven—but the benefits of this appliance don't stop there. Here are a few more reasons to switch to air frying:

It replaces other cooking appliances. Thanks to its quicker cooking times, the air fryer is the perfect alternative to your oven—but it can also replace your deep fryer, dehydrator, and microwave! In one device, you'll be able to whip up perfect meals, snacks, sides, and more without sacrificing any of the flavor.

It uses little to no cooking oil. Traditionally cooked fried foods are prepared by submerging foods in heated oil, which means they are high in bad fats and calories. Also, when oil is heated beyond its smoking point, as with deep frying, it can produce toxic fumes and free radicals. The air fryer drastically cuts down on fatty oils, meaning more nutritious meals. This can also lead to weight loss and better overall health.

It makes vegetables appeal to the pickiest eaters. Picky vegetable eaters (or parents of picky vegetable eaters) can benefit from the transformative ways of the air fryer. A little gluten-free breading and a fresh dipping sauce turn that zucchini into tasty fries! Also, a little cornflake breading on some cod can be your gateway recipe from fish sticks to a salmon fillet.

BREAD CRUMB OPTIONS

If you are following a gluten-free diet, your bread crumb world is certainly not limited. And although there are ready-made gluten-free bread crumb options, you can easily make your own with gluten-free cookies, chips, crackers, and even cereal. Simply smash them down to the desired consistency and bread away!

Purchasing an Air Fryer

There are several brands, sizes, and temperature ranges of air fryers on the market. This book is based on a four-person air fryer with a 1-pound, 13-ounce capacity and 1,425 watts. If you're looking to cook meals to feed a family, you might be interested in a 5.3-quart fryer that can be used to roast an entire chicken, but if you want a small machine because of limited kitchen space and you're cooking for only one or two people, you can crisp up savory Eggplant Parmesan Fries (see Chapter 3) with a smaller model. As for the temperature range, some air fryers allow you to dehydrate foods because you can cook them at a very low temperature for a long period of time. Depending on the functions you need, you'll want to make sure your air fryer has the appropriate cooking capacity and temperature range.

AVOIDING OILS DIRECTLY ON THE AIR FRYER BASKET

If you want to cut back on oil even more, instead of giving your basket a light spray or brush of oil, simply cut a piece of parchment paper to the size of the bottom of your air fryer basket. It will help keep the batter on your items without adding additional calories.

Air Fryer Functions

Settings can vary between different air fryer models on the market. Some of the newer types offer digital settings to control the temperature and time, while others have analog dials as well as preset temperatures for certain fresh and frozen foods. All recipes in this book were created using manual times and temperatures. Every air fryer allows you to set these yourself. Still, it is important to know how the cooking programs work on your air fryer and when to use them. And although some brands will claim you don't need to preheat the air fryer, skipping this step can alter cooking times. The recipes in this book include preheating instructions.

HEATING FROZEN FOODS

Many quick and/or gluten-free options are in the frozen food sections, but while the microwave is fast, frozen foods never quite come out as well as you would like. The air fryer creates a perfect crunchy exterior, and brings out the flavors that are lacking in microwaved meals.

In addition, because the air fryer basket is going to be used when making most of your air-fried foods, finding a model with a quick-release button will make your life easier. This button releases the fryer basket containing food from the bottom basket so you can shake or flip the food with ease.

Air Fryer Accessories

The air fryer comes with an air fryer basket; however, there are many other recipes that can be made with the purchase of a few additional accessories. Before you purchase any of these, check that they work with your size and brand of air fryer. Here are some of the common air fryer accessories:

Metal holder. This round rack allows for a second layer of food in the air fryer so you can maximize space and cook multiple foods at once.

Skewer rack. This is similar to a metal holder, but it also contains four metal skewers for roasting meat and vegetable kebabs.

Ramekin. Small ramekins are great for making mini cakes and quiches. If they're oven-safe, they're safe to use in your air fryer.

Cake barrel. You can find both round and square versions. As a bonus, they also have a handle that makes retrieving the barrel from the air fryer a cinch.

Cupcake pan. This pan usually comes with seven silicone cupcake liners (also called baking cups) that are oven-safe and great for mini meatloaves, cupcakes, on-the-go frittatas, little quick breads, and muffins.

They are reusable and dishwasher-safe, making cleanup a snap!

Parchment. Specially pre-cut parchment makes cleanup even easier when baking with your air fryer. You can also find parchment paper with pre-cut holes for steaming.

Pizza pan. This shallow nonstick pan allows you to make mini pizzas and also provides a flat surface for a variety of other recipes, such as biscuits, Dutch pancakes, and the delectable Amaretto Cheesecake found in Chapter 9!

Grill pan. This replaces the air fryer basket and is used for grilling fish, meat, and vegetables, and baking certain desserts, such as pavlova.

Accessory Removal

When cooking pot-in-appliance, you'll want to be careful to avoid burning yourself once it's time to remove the inserted dish. Here are a few useful tools for safely removing items from your air fryer:

Tongs. Wooden or silicone-tipped tongs will allow you to safely remove pans that don't have handles. They will also help you to flip food items such as meat.

Oven mitts. Because of the tight space, it is almost impossible to use thick oven mitts to grip accessories in the air fryer. Heat-resistant mini mitts or pinch mitts are small food-grade silicone oven mitts that will allow you to lift pots out of the fryer safely after the cooking process.

ACCESSORY REMOVAL HACK
You can also create an aluminum foil sling to lift a heated dish out of the air fryer. Simply fold a 10" × 10" square of aluminum foil in half, then fold again lengthwise. Place the sling underneath the bowl or pan before cooking.

Cleaning and Seasoning Your Air Fryer

After using your air fryer, it is important to unplug the appliance and allow it to completely cool before cleaning. Adding cooler water to a hot fryer basket can cause warping. Although the removable parts are dishwasher-safe, washing them by hand can lengthen the life of the coated nonstick parts. To clean the air fryer pan you'll need to:

1. Remove the air fryer pan from the base. Fill the pan with hot water and dish soap. Let the pan soak with the frying basket inside for 10 minutes.

2. Clean the basket thoroughly with a sponge or brush.

3. Remove the fryer basket and scrub the underside and outside walls.

4. Clean the air fryer pan with a sponge or brush.

5. Let everything air-dry and return to the air fryer base.

6. Wipe the outside of the air fryer base with a damp cloth.

Once dry, the fryer basket can also be seasoned. You may have heard this term with cast iron pans, but the air fryer basket can benefit from seasoning as well. Preheat the air fryer with the basket for 5 minutes at 400°F. Remove the basket and when cool enough to touch, spread a thin layer of coconut oil on the inside using a paper towel. Then simply heat the basket for an additional 2 minutes. This will help extend the life of the nonstick coating in the basket.

What Is Gluten?

Simply put, gluten is the protein found in wheat, rye, spelt, and barley. It acts as a glue to hold ingredients together in products like bread, pasta, and tortillas. And while these are the products most people think of when they hear the word "gluten," you may be surprised to learn that it is often also hidden in the following everyday food items:

- Condiments such as soy sauce, ketchup, and mustard
- Sauces
- Processed meats
- Coffee substitutes
- Beer
- Soups (especially cream-based)

In these products, gluten is most commonly used as either a filler or stabilizer for a longer shelf life.

Living the Gluten-Free Lifestyle

There are many reasons to go gluten-free! For more than three million people, this decision stems from an allergy known as celiac disease, which triggers negative physical reactions to gluten. Others decide to eliminate gluten because of the many positive side effects. For example, ridding your body of gluten assists in stomach issues such as gas, bloating, and leaky gut syndrome. The gluten-free lifestyle also means eliminating many processed foods, which can result in weight loss, increased energy levels, and better sleep. Reduced inflammation (or risk of inflammation) is another great side effect of eating gluten-free, and arthritis, allergy symptoms, and other ailments linked to inflammation can be alleviated. You can learn more from your doctor about how the gluten-free lifestyle might be beneficial for you!

Tips to Remember

Keep the following tips in mind as you plan your gluten-free meals:

Always read labels. To avoid consuming products that may contain gluten, always look at labels before you make a purchase. Some ingredients (including those used in recipes in this book) have both gluten-free and gluten-containing options available, so checking the label ensures that your selection is gluten-free. Ingredients to be especially mindful of include mayonnaise, beer, hot sauce, horseradish, processed meats, and salad dressings.

Items that are truly gluten-free will usually also have a certified seal somewhere on the packaging.

Focus on what you *can* eat. There is a whole host of great gluten-free products and meals on the market today, so don't think of the gluten-free lifestyle as a restriction: think of it as an opportunity to expand your palate!

Get creative. Don't fall into the trap of only eating meat and vegetables to avoid gluten. Again, there is a lot available to you, so try out different recipes, and even create your own new dishes for variety.

Now that you have a better understanding of your air fryer and the gluten-free diet, it's time to get cooking! The easy recipes in this book are a great starting point for your journey, or the perfect inspiration if you've been stuck rotating through the same meals each week. Feel free to customize dishes to your liking, but be sure to check that any additions are truly gluten-free.

Breakfast and Gluten-Free Breads

Fitting breakfast into a hectic schedule can seem a bit overwhelming at times, especially if you are following a gluten-free diet. You will oftentimes have to make your own breakfasts because there are so many gluten-filled fast foods, including hidden sources of gluten in a variety of sauces such as salad dressing and barbecue sauce. The air fryer can help save the day with its shortened cooking time and freedom from having to stand over the skillet.

Many breakfast options in the gluten-free lifestyle can also seem repetitive. From eggs to muffins, this chapter offers a wide variety of delicious breakfast and bread recipes, including Pimiento Cheesy Tots, Green Eggs and Ham Breakfast Sandwiches, and Salted Caramel Banana Muffins. Breakfast will never be boring again! And once you get comfortable with the basics, you should feel free to be creative and make your own morning masterpieces. So get cooking, and let your family wake up with a new appreciation for their favorite (or at least soon-to-be favorite) kitchen appliance!

Sage Sausage Patties

Making your own sausage is actually quite easy, and it ensures that you know exactly what is going into the filling. The sage and touch of nutmeg lend an autumnal feel to these tasty Sage Sausage Patties.

- **Hands-On Time:** 10 minutes
- **Cook Time:** 20 minutes

Serves 4

12 ounces ground pork

¼ cup finely diced peeled yellow onion

1 teaspoon rubbed sage

1 tablespoon light brown sugar

⅛ teaspoon ground nutmeg

¼ teaspoon salt

¼ teaspoon ground black pepper

1 tablespoon water

GRINDING YOUR OWN SAUSAGE

If you are really adventurous, try grinding your own meat. This way, the sausage can be made in larger batches and frozen for future morning meals!

1 Preheat air fryer at 350°F for 3 minutes.

2 Combine pork, onion, sage, brown sugar, nutmeg, salt, and pepper in a large bowl. Form mixture into eight patties.

3 Pour water into bottom of air fryer. Place four patties in air fryer basket lightly greased with preferred cooking oil and cook 5 minutes. Flip patties. Cook an additional 5 minutes. Repeat with remaining patties.

4 Transfer patties to a large plate and serve warm.

Pimiento Cheesy Tots

To cut down the cook time of these crispy and creamy tots even further, use leftover mashed potatoes (about 2 cups). This recipe is great for breakfast, a side, or a snack!

- **Hands-On Time:** 15 minutes
- **Cook Time:** 90 minutes

Serves 4

2 medium russet potatoes, scrubbed

1 tablespoon olive oil

2 tablespoons butter, room temperature

4 tablespoons finely diced peeled yellow onion

½ cup pimento cheese

2 tablespoons gluten-free all-purpose flour

1 teaspoon salt

½ teaspoon ground black pepper

HOW TO MAKE PIMENTO CHEESE

Although prepared pimento cheese can be purchased in the deli section of most grocery stores, making it couldn't be any easier! In a medium bowl combine 16 ounces finely shredded Cheddar cheese, 1 (4-ounce) jar pimentos including juice, ½ cup mayonnaise, ¼ teaspoon salt, and ¼ teaspoon freshly ground black pepper. Refrigerate covered for up to two days until ready to use.

1 Preheat air fryer at 400°F for 3 minutes.

2 Prick each potato four times with tines of a fork. Rub olive oil evenly over potatoes. Place in ungreased air fryer basket.

3 Cook potatoes 45 minutes. Once done, transfer to a plate and let rest about 10 minutes until cool enough to handle.

4 Scoop cooled potato flesh into a medium bowl. Discard skins. Add butter, onion, pimento cheese, flour, salt, and pepper. Using back of a fork, smash together ingredients until smooth.

5 Tightly form a tablespoon-sized amount of potato mixture into a tot shape. Repeat twenty-four times with remaining mixture.

6 Add one-third of tots to air fryer basket lightly greased with preferred cooking oil. Brush tots with oil. Cook 15 minutes. Transfer to a plate and repeat two more times with remaining tots.

7 Let cooked tots sit 3 minutes until cool enough to handle. Use fingers to press cooled tots back into shape. Serve warm.

Perfect Hard-"Boiled" Eggs

The air fryer provides a supereasy method to hard-boil eggs without having to deal with splashing boiling water.

- **Hands-On Time: 5 minutes**
- **Cook Time: 15 minutes**

Serves 8

8 large eggs, in shell
1 cup ice cubes
2 cups water

1   Preheat air fryer at 250°F for 3 minutes.

2   Add eggs to ungreased air fryer basket. Cook 15 minutes.

3   Add ice and water to a large bowl. Transfer cooked eggs to this water bath immediately to stop cooking process. Let sit 5 minutes, then peel and eat.

Sunrise Deviled Eggs

Serve these tasty eggs with a side of fresh melon and a slice of gluten-free bread. Make them ahead of time for a quick grab in the morning (hopefully they'll make it to breakfast!).

- **Hands-On Time: 5 minutes**
- **Cook Time: 15 minutes**

Serves 4

4 large eggs
1 cup ice cubes
1 cup water
2 tablespoons mayonnaise
1 teaspoon yellow mustard
½ teaspoon dill pickle juice
1 teaspoon finely diced sweet pickles
⅛ teaspoon salt
⅛ teaspoon ground black pepper
2 tablespoons finely grated Cheddar cheese
2 slices cooked bacon, crumbled

1   Preheat air fryer at 250°F for 3 minutes.

2   Add eggs to ungreased air fryer basket. Cook 15 minutes.

3   Add ice and water to a medium bowl. Transfer cooked eggs to this water bath immediately to stop cooking process. Let sit 5 minutes, then carefully peel eggs.

4   Cut eggs in half lengthwise. Spoon yolks into a medium bowl. Arrange egg white halves on a medium plate.

5   Using a fork, blend egg yolks with mayonnaise, mustard, pickle juice, pickles, salt, and pepper. Fold in cheese. Spoon mixture into egg white halves. Garnish with crumbled bacon and serve.

Green Eggs and Ham Breakfast Sandwiches

Would you eat these in a box? Would you eat these with a fox? Sam-I-Am sure would! But shhh: the eggs aren't really green. The pesto not only adds the classic green color, but also the flavor that makes these sandwiches undeniably delicious.

- **Hands-On Time:** 10 minutes
- **Cook Time:** 6 minutes

Serves 2

- 4 slices gluten-free sandwich bread
- 2 tablespoons butter, melted and divided
- 4 large eggs, scrambled
- 4 slices deli ham
- 2 slices Colby cheese
- 4 teaspoons basil pesto sauce

1 Preheat air fryer at 375°F for 3 minutes.

2 Brush two pieces gluten-free bread with half of butter and place butter side down into ungreased air fryer basket. Divide eggs, ham, and cheese evenly on each bread slice in basket.

3 Spread pesto on remaining bread slices and place slices pesto side down onto sandwiches in basket. Brush remaining butter on tops of sandwiches.

4 Cook 3 minutes. Flip, then cook an additional 3 minutes. Serve warm.

Cinnamon Sugar Toast

This kid-friendly and fun breakfast toast is so easy to make in the air fryer. The fryer crisps the bottom and top of the bread, while the butter, cinnamon, and sugar heat to magical perfection.

- **Hands-On Time:** 10 minutes
- **Cook Time:** 8 minutes

Serves 2

¼ cup granulated sugar

1½ teaspoons ground cinnamon

2 tablespoons butter, room temperature

4 slices gluten-free sandwich bread

1 In a small bowl, combine sugar and cinnamon.

2 Preheat air fryer at 375°F for 3 minutes.

3 Spread butter over bread slices. Evenly sprinkle buttered slices with cinnamon-sugar mix.

4 Place two bread slices in ungreased air fryer basket and cook 4 minutes. Transfer to a large plate. Repeat with remaining slices. Serve warm.

Rainbow French Toast Sticks

It's true! Fruity Pebbles are gluten-free and they make the most colorful French toast sticks. This isn't exactly a healthy breakfast option, but fun can be had on some days!

- **Hands-On Time:** 10 minutes
- **Cook Time:** 10 minutes

Yields 16 sticks

1 large egg

⅓ cup whole milk

⅛ teaspoon salt

½ teaspoon ground cinnamon

1 cup crushed Post Fruity Pebbles cereal

4 slices gluten-free sandwich bread, each cut into 4 sticks

¼ cup pure maple syrup

1 Preheat air fryer at 375°F for 3 minutes.

2 In a small bowl, whisk together egg, milk, salt, and cinnamon. Place cereal crumbs in a small shallow dish.

3 Dip bread sticks in egg mixture. Dredge in cereal crumbs.

4 Place half of bread sticks in air fryer basket lightly greased with preferred cooking oil. Cook 3 minutes. Flip, then cook an additional 2 minutes. Repeat with remaining bread sticks.

5 Transfer sticks to a large plate and serve warm with maple syrup to dip.

Lox and Avocado Toast

There is a reason that avocado toast has become more and more popular over the years: it is delicious and full of fiber and healthy fat. Add different traditional bagel ingredients to discover your new favorite!

- **Hands-On Time:** 10 minutes
- **Cook Time:** 10 minutes

Serves 2

1 medium avocado, peeled and pitted

1 clove garlic, peeled and minced

¼ teaspoon lime juice

⅛ teaspoon salt

2 slices gluten-free bread

2 medium Campari tomatoes, sliced

¼ teaspoon ground black pepper

4 ounces smoked salmon

2 tablespoons capers

2 tablespoons diced peeled red onion

1 Preheat air fryer at 350°F for 3 minutes.

2 In a small bowl, use the back of a fork to press avocado flesh, garlic, lime juice, and salt until desired consistency is reached.

3 Spread avocado mixture on bread slices. Add tomato slices. Sprinkle with black pepper.

4 Place topped bread in ungreased air fryer basket. Cook 5 minutes. Transfer to a plate. Repeat with remaining bread. Top each piece of bread with salmon, capers, and red onion. Serve warm.

WHAT ARE CAMPARI TOMATOES?
You may have noticed Campari tomatoes in your local grocery store, and they are definitely worth a try. Larger than cherry tomatoes and smaller than Roma tomatoes, they are grown hydroponically in water. So sweet and deep red in color, they are delicious and eye-catching in recipes and garnishes.

"Quiche Lorraine" Egg Cups

Quiche usually has a buttery pie crust, which means gluten sensitivities don't always agree with this breakfast favorite. Luckily, these portable egg cups have all of the traditional fillings of cheese, cream, and bacon—without the gluten!

- **Hands-On Time:** 10 minutes
- **Cook Time:** 18 minutes

Serves 6

3 large eggs
2 tablespoons half-and-half
⅛ teaspoon salt
⅛ teaspoon ground black pepper
2 tablespoons finely diced peeled white onion
3 slices cooked bacon, crumbled
¼ cup shredded Swiss cheese
1 medium Roma tomato, cut into 6 thin slices

1 Preheat air fryer at 350°F for 3 minutes.

2 In a small bowl, whisk together eggs, half-and-half, salt, and pepper.

3 Evenly distribute onion, bacon, and cheese among six silicone cupcake liners lightly greased with preferred cooking oil. Pour whisked eggs into cupcake liners. Top each cup with one tomato slice.

4 Place three cups in air fryer basket and cook 9 minutes. Transfer to a large plate and repeat with remaining egg cups. Serve warm.

Tater Tot Egg Cups

Although it seems that all Tater Tots should be naturally gluten-free since they are just potato, do your due diligence by researching brands before you make a purchase. Most have received the gluten-free label during testing, but there are a few brands that aren't certified!

- **Hands-On Time:** 15 minutes
- **Cook Time:** 28 minutes

Serves 4

32 gluten-free Tater Tots, frozen
4 large eggs
½ teaspoon salt
½ teaspoon ground black pepper
4 slices cooked bacon, crumbled
¼ cup finely shredded Cheddar cheese

COOKING FROZEN TATER TOTS IN AN AIR FRYER
Cooking these little cuties to add to your breakfast table couldn't be any easier, thanks to the air fryer. Preheat air fryer to 400°F for 3 minutes. Place a layer of tots in air fryer basket lightly greased with preferred cooking oil. Cook 6 minutes. Shake basket, then cook an additional 6 minutes. Tot sizes may vary between brands, so check the tots after 10 minutes of cooking.

1 Preheat air fryer to 400°F for 3 minutes.

2 Divide tots into eight silicone cupcake liners (four tots per cup). Place four cupcake liners in air fryer basket and cook 4 minutes.

3 Once done, use the back of a spoon to smoosh tots in each cup down into an even crust. Cook an additional 5 minutes. Repeat cooking steps with remaining cupcake liners.

4 In a medium bowl, whisk together eggs, salt, and pepper.

5 Evenly distribute bacon and cheese among cooked cupcake liners. Pour egg mixture into cups and cook cups (four at a time) in air fryer 5 minutes. Remove from basket and serve warm.

Spinach and Goat Cheese Frittata (pictured)

Serve this light and tasty brunch dish for two on a lazy morning. To make it even better, add some bacon, avocado slices, or even a dollop of sour cream.

- **Hands-On Time:** 10 minutes
- **Cook Time:** 14 minutes

Serves 2

5 large eggs
¼ teaspoon salt
¼ teaspoon ground black pepper
½ cup baby spinach leaves
1 large shallot, peeled and diced

1 Preheat air fryer at 325°F for 3 minutes.

2 In a medium bowl, whisk together eggs, salt, and pepper. Stir in remaining ingredients. Pour into a round 7" cake barrel lightly greased with preferred cooking oil.

3 Place barrel in air fryer basket and cook 14 minutes. Once done, transfer to a cooling rack to sit 5 minutes. Slice and serve warm.

Ham and Cheddar Strata

Strata is similar to quiche in that it has an egg filling; however, unlike with the quiche, the strata doesn't have a pie crust. The strata also contains pieces of bread to give it a starchy feel. In this recipe, the eggs create a savory, protein-filled dish with the texture of bread pudding.

- **Hands-On Time:** 10 minutes
- **Cook Time:** 14 minutes

Serves 4

5 large eggs
¼ teaspoon salt
¼ teaspoon ground black pepper
1 teaspoon Dijon mustard
¼ cup minced peeled sweet yellow onion
¼ cup small-diced cooked ham
⅓ cup shredded Cheddar cheese
2 pieces gluten-free sandwich bread, diced

1 Preheat air fryer at 325°F for 3 minutes.

2 In a medium bowl, whisk eggs. Stir in remaining ingredients. Pour into a round 7" cake barrel lightly greased with preferred cooking oil.

3 Place barrel in air fryer basket and cook 14 minutes. Once done, transfer to a cooling rack to sit 5 minutes. Slice and serve warm.

Cinnamon Raisin Rice Cereal

Whether you eat a bowl of this cereal with milk or just take it along dry as a snack in the car, give this delicious recipe a try!

- **Hands-On Time:** 10 minutes
- **Cook Time:** 5 minutes

Serves 4

4 cups gluten-free rice cereal

1 cup unsweetened coconut shreds

¼ cup raisins

2 tablespoons creamy peanut butter

1 teaspoon vanilla extract

¼ cup pure maple syrup

1 tablespoon light brown sugar

2 teaspoons ground cinnamon

¼ cup almond flour

⅛ teaspoon salt

1 Preheat air fryer at 350°F for 3 minutes.

2 In a medium bowl, combine all ingredients. Press mixture into a 7" cake barrel lightly greased with preferred cooking oil.

3 Place barrel in air fryer basket and cook 3 minutes. Stir ingredients, then cook an additional 2 minutes.

4 Once done let cool completely, about 10 minutes. Crumble into an airtight container until ready to serve, up to five days.

Chocolate Hazelnut Granola

This recipe calls for hazelnut flour, but you can use almond or coconut flour if that is what you have on hand.

- **Hands-On Time:** 5 minutes
- **Cook Time:** 5 minutes

Serves 4

1 cup chopped pecans
1 cup quick-cooking oats
1 tablespoon chia seeds
1 tablespoon flaxseed
1 cup unsweetened coconut shreds
¼ cup chocolate hazelnut spread
¼ cup diced pitted dates
¼ cup honey
1 tablespoon light brown sugar
½ teaspoon vanilla extract
¼ cup hazelnut flour
2 tablespoons unsweetened powdered chocolate
⅛ teaspoon salt

1 Preheat air fryer at 350°F for 3 minutes.

2 In a medium bowl, combine all ingredients. Press mixture into a 7" cake barrel lightly greased with preferred cooking oil.

3 Place barrel in air fryer basket and cook 3 minutes. Stir ingredients, then cook an additional 2 minutes.

4 Once done let cool completely, about 10 minutes. Crumble into an airtight container until ready to serve, up to five days.

MAKE YOUR OWN NUT FLOUR
Although sold commercially, nut meals and flours can be a little pricey. But I'll share a secret with you: the only ingredient you need to make your own is your choice of nut. Simply throw a handful in the food processor and pulse to your desired consistency. Just don't pulse for too long, as you'll create a nut butter!

Pumpkin Cereal

With a limited supply of gluten-free cereals available on store shelves, take matters into your own hands. Homemade cereal allows you to choose flavors and gives you control over the ingredients.

- **Hands-On Time:** 5 minutes
- **Cook Time:** 5 minutes

Serves 4

1 cup unsalted pumpkin seeds

⅔ cup chopped pecans

⅓ cup quick-cooking oats

1 cup unsweetened coconut shreds

¼ cup pumpkin purée

¼ cup diced pitted dates

2 tablespoons almond butter

2 teaspoons pumpkin pie spice

¼ cup honey

1 tablespoon dark brown sugar

¼ cup coconut flour

⅛ teaspoon salt

1 Preheat air fryer at 350°F for 3 minutes.

2 In a medium bowl, combine all ingredients. Press mixture into a 7″ cake barrel lightly greased with preferred cooking oil.

3 Place barrel in air fryer basket and cook 3 minutes. Stir ingredients, then cook an additional 2 minutes.

4 Once done let cool completely, about 10 minutes. Crumble into a large airtight container until ready to serve, up to five days.

THE DIFFERENCE BETWEEN LIGHT AND DARK BROWN SUGAR

While these sugars can be interchangeable in recipes, know that there is a slight difference between them. Both are flavored with molasses; however, dark brown sugar contains more, which leads to a richer, more acidic taste.

Trail Mix Oatmeal

When you are on the go, this trail mix will fill you with nutrition and warmth. It is also great served warm in a bowl with some milk.

- **Hands-On Time:** 10 minutes
- **Cook Time:** 8 minutes

Serves 4

1½ cups quick-cooking oats

⅓ cup light brown sugar

1 large egg

1 teaspoon orange zest

1 tablespoon fresh-squeezed orange juice

2 tablespoons whole milk

2 tablespoons pure maple syrup

2 tablespoons unsalted butter, melted

2 tablespoons raisins

2 tablespoons dried cranberries

⅛ teaspoon ground nutmeg

⅛ teaspoon salt

¼ cup pecan pieces

¼ cup mini chocolate chips

1 Preheat air fryer at 325°F for 3 minutes.

2 In a medium bowl, combine all ingredients except mini chocolate chips. Transfer mixture to a 7″ cake barrel lightly greased with preferred cooking oil.

3 Place barrel in air fryer basket and cook 8 minutes.

4 Once done, transfer to a cooling rack and let sit 5 minutes. Slice and serve warm garnished with chocolate chips.

Loaded Breakfast Quesadillas

This is an easy breakfast to make, and can be catered to each member of the family. Add your own ingredients to change up the flavors. You can serve this dish as is, or with fresh guacamole or salsa for a twist!

- **Hands-On Time:** 10 minutes
- **Cook Time:** 16 minutes

Serves 4

8 (6") gluten-free flour tortillas

½ pound cooked bacon, crumbled

6 large eggs, scrambled

1½ cups shredded Cheddar cheese

1 Preheat air fryer to 350°F for 3 minutes.

2 Place one tortilla in bottom of an ungreased 7" round cake barrel. Evenly layer one-quarter portion each of bacon, eggs, and cheese over tortilla. Top with second tortilla.

3 Place barrel in air fryer basket and cook 4 minutes, then transfer to a large plate. Repeat with remaining tortillas and ingredients.

4 Let quesadillas cool 3 minutes, then slice and serve.

Buttermilk Biscuits

Sometimes it is lonely when you have to eat gluten-free while everyone else is sopping up gravy with their biscuits. Well, guess what? You can now have delicious biscuits too!

- **Hands-On Time:** 10 minutes
- **Cook Time:** 16 minutes

Serves 4

2 cups gluten-free all-purpose flour

1 tablespoon baking powder

½ teaspoon baking soda

½ teaspoon xanthan gum

½ teaspoon salt

½ teaspoon granulated sugar

4 tablespoons butter, cold, cubed

1¼ cups buttermilk

1 In a small bowl, combine flour, baking powder, baking soda, xanthan gum, salt, and sugar. Add butter and buttermilk gradually until a sticky dough forms.

2 Preheat air fryer at 350°F for 3 minutes.

3 Flour your hands and form dough into eight balls. Add four balls to a pizza pan lightly greased with preferred cooking oil. Biscuits will be touching.

4 Place pan in air fryer basket and cook biscuits 8 minutes. Repeat with remaining four biscuits.

5 Transfer biscuits to a large plate. Serve warm.

Corn Dog Muffins

Enjoy these little Corn Dog Muffins for breakfast on the go, as a snack, or even for game day! You can now enjoy this fan favorite without the deep frying. And, because they don't come on a pointy stick, they are safe for the youngsters too!

- **Hands-On Time:** 10 minutes
- **Cook Time:** 18 minutes

Serves 8

1 cup Bob's Red Mill Gluten Free Cornbread Mix

2 teaspoons granulated sugar

⅛ teaspoon salt

¾ cup buttermilk

3 tablespoons butter, melted

1 large egg

¼ cup minced peeled yellow onion

2 beef hot dogs, sliced and cut into half-moons

1 Preheat air fryer at 350°F for 3 minutes.

2 In a small bowl, combine cornbread mix, sugar, and salt. In another small bowl, whisk together buttermilk, butter, and egg. Add wet ingredients to dry ingredients and combine. Fold in minced onion and hot dog pieces. Transfer to eight silicone cupcake liners lightly greased with preferred cooking oil.

3 Place four cupcake liners in air fryer basket and cook 9 minutes. Repeat with remaining cupcake liners. Serve warm.

Salted Caramel Banana Muffins

Enjoy these muffins with a cup of tea for a relaxing breakfast, or with some coffee on the go during a chaotic morning. If you can't find salted caramel chips, substitute with your favorite flavor, such as white chocolate, butterscotch, or peanut butter. Any flavor will work wonderfully with the banana base.

- **Hands-On Time:** 10 minutes
- **Cook Time:** 14 minutes

Serves 8

1 cup gluten-free all-purpose flour
½ teaspoon baking soda
⅓ cup granulated sugar
¼ teaspoon salt
⅓ cup mashed banana, about 1 large ripe banana
½ teaspoon vanilla extract
1 large egg
1 tablespoon vegetable oil
¼ cup salted caramel chips

1 Preheat air fryer at 375°F for 3 minutes.

2 In a large bowl, combine flour, baking soda, sugar, and salt. In a separate medium bowl, combine mashed banana, vanilla, egg, and oil.

3 Pour wet ingredients into dry ingredients and gently combine. Fold in salted caramel chips. Do not overmix. Spoon mixture into eight silicone cupcake liners lightly greased with preferred cooking oil.

4 Place four muffins in air fryer basket. Cook 7 minutes, then transfer to a cooling rack. Repeat with remaining muffins. Serve warm or cooled.

Lemon Blueberry Muffins

The beautiful combination of lemon and blueberry is such a traditional delight. The citrus freshness marries nicely with the tartness of the blueberries. For a dessert option, add a light glaze and enjoy your muffins with a cup of tea to end a long day.

- **Hands-On Time:** 10 minutes
- **Cook Time:** 14 minutes

Serves 8

1 cup gluten-free all-purpose flour
½ teaspoon baking soda
⅓ cup granulated sugar
¼ teaspoon salt
1 tablespoon unsweetened applesauce
1 tablespoon lemon juice
1 teaspoon lemon zest
½ teaspoon vanilla extract
1 large egg
1 tablespoon vegetable oil
¼ cup halved fresh blueberries

1 Preheat air fryer at 375°F for 3 minutes.

2 In a large bowl, combine flour, baking soda, sugar, and salt.

3 In a medium bowl, combine applesauce, lemon juice, lemon zest, vanilla, egg, and oil.

4 Pour wet ingredients from medium bowl into large bowl with dry ingredients. Gently combine. Fold in blueberries. Do not overmix. Spoon mixture into eight silicone cupcake liners lightly greased with preferred cooking oil.

5 Place four muffins in air fryer basket. Cook 7 minutes, then transfer to a cooling rack. Repeat with remaining muffins. Serve warm or cooled.

Toffee Chocolate Chip Zucchini Bread

I double-dog dare you to tell the difference between this zucchini bread and your favorite banana bread. And the addition of toffee bits and chocolate chips?! Yes, please. Zucchini not only lends a moistness to the bread, but it is also packed with vitamins A and C, along with fiber and potassium.

- **Hands-On Time: 10 minutes**
- **Cook Time: 20 minutes**

Serves 6

1 cup gluten-free all-purpose flour
½ teaspoon baking soda
½ cup granulated sugar
¼ teaspoon ground cinnamon
¼ teaspoon salt
⅓ cup grated zucchini
1 large egg
1 tablespoon olive oil
1 teaspoon vanilla extract
2 tablespoons English toffee bits
2 tablespoons mini chocolate chips

1 Preheat air fryer at 375°F for 3 minutes.

2 In a medium bowl, combine all ingredients. Pour mixture into a 7" springform pan lightly greased with preferred cooking oil.

3 Place springform pan in air fryer basket. Cook 20 minutes.

4 Remove pan from air fryer and let cool 10 minutes to set.

5 Once cooled, remove springform sides. Slice and serve warm.

SUBSTITUTING CHOCOLATE TOFFEE CHIPS
If you can't find English toffee bits for this recipe, there are also chocolate toffee chips available at most grocery stores. Simply replace the toffee bits with 4 tablespoons of chocolate toffee chips.

Nutty Butternut Squash Bread

Although this recipe uses canned butternut squash purée, you can easily make your own for an even fresher taste. Check out the Butternut Squash Purée in Chapter 4 for instructions.

- **Hands-On Time:** 10 minutes
- **Cook Time:** 20 minutes

Serves 8

1 cup gluten-free all-purpose flour
½ teaspoon baking soda
½ cup granulated sugar
1 teaspoon ground cinnamon
1 teaspoon pumpkin pie spice
¼ teaspoon salt
½ cup canned butternut squash purée
1 large egg
1 tablespoon vegetable oil
1 tablespoon orange juice
1 teaspoon orange zest
¼ cup crushed walnuts

1 Preheat air fryer at 375°F for 3 minutes.

2 In a medium bowl, combine all ingredients. Pour mixture into a 7" springform pan lightly greased with preferred cooking oil.

3 Place springform pan in air fryer basket. Cook 20 minutes.

4 Remove from air fryer and let cool 10 minutes to set. Once set, remove springform sides. Slice and serve warm.

3

Appetizers, Snacks, and Dipping Sauces

Living within certain diet requirements is never harder than when you are with a group of friends. Chips and dips and deep-fried, breaded everything seem to swarm the tables. But hunger or plates of boring, unhealthy food don't have to be your only options. Use the air fryer to create a healthy gluten-free option to share. Or, better yet, throw your own shindig and show folks what they've been missing! Appetizers are a great way to bring a group of people together to enjoy a game, or to hold them over until you serve a meal.

Quick, crispy food air fried in minutes? Now that's how you throw a party! With amazing appetizers ranging from Dill Pickle Chips and Trail Mix Chex Snack, to Honey Mustard Wings and Reuben Deviled Eggs, the only problem you'll have incorporating the recipes in this chapter into your next social event will be deciding which ones to make. And after the appetizers have been devoured, make a batch of Sriracha Mayonnaise to drizzle on gluten-free taco entrées or use as a dip for your air-fried vegetable side dishes. Your friends and family won't even know that they are eating gluten-free food!

Creamy Black Olive–Stuffed Jalapeños

The mild flavors of the cheese and black olives tame the heat of the jalapeños. However, if you want to step things up, stir the jalapeño seeds into the cheese mixture.

- **Hands-On Time:** 10 minutes
- **Cook Time:** 8 minutes

Serves 5

¼ cup plain cream cheese, room temperature

¼ cup finely grated Cheddar cheese

2 tablespoons chopped black olives

5 medium jalapeño peppers, cut lengthwise, seeded

1 Preheat air fryer at 350°F for 3 minutes.

2 In a small bowl, cream together cream cheese, Cheddar cheese, and black olives.

3 Press cream cheese mixture into each jalapeño half.

4 Lay stuffed peppers in ungreased air fryer basket. Cook 8 minutes.

5 Once done, transfer stuffed peppers to a medium serving plate and serve warm.

After-School Taquito Quesadillas

It just doesn't get any easier than this recipe. Usually taquitos are corn tortillas that are filled, rolled up, and fried. This version simplifies things by turning the taquitos into a simple cheese quesadilla. If you have leftover chicken or a can of sliced olives, go ahead and add them in! Also, try serving with salsa, sour cream, or guacamole for a tasty dip.

- **Hands-On Time:** 10 minutes
- **Cook Time:** 24 minutes

Serves 4

8 tablespoons Mexican blend shredded cheese

8 (6") soft corn tortillas

2 teaspoons olive oil

1 Preheat air fryer at 350°F for 3 minutes.

2 Evenly sprinkle cheese over four tortillas. Top each with a remaining tortilla and brush the tops lightly with oil.

3 Place one quesadilla in ungreased air fryer basket. Cook 6 minutes. Remove and repeat with remaining quesadillas.

4 Transfer quesadillas to a large serving tray and serve warm.

Reuben Deviled Eggs

The traditional Reuben sandwich is an American grilled delicacy, but the flavors don't just have to be celebrated between two slices of gluten-filled bread. Check out these scrumptious Reuben Deviled Eggs for a twist on two classics: the Reuben and the deviled egg!

- **Hands-On Time:** 5 minutes
- **Cook Time:** 15 minutes

Serves 4

4 large eggs
1 cup ice cubes
1 cup water
2 tablespoons mayonnaise
1 tablespoon Thousand Island dressing
⅛ teaspoon salt
⅛ teaspoon ground black pepper
2 tablespoons finely chopped corned beef
1 teaspoon caraway seeds
2 tablespoons finely chopped Swiss cheese

1 Preheat air fryer at 250°F for 3 minutes.

2 Place eggs in silicone cupcake liners to avoid eggs from moving around or cracking during cooking process. Add silicone cups to air fryer basket. Cook 15 minutes.

3 Add ice and water to a medium bowl. Transfer cooked eggs to water bath immediately to stop cooking process. After 5 minutes, carefully peel eggs.

4 Cut eggs in half lengthwise. Spoon yolks into a medium bowl. Arrange white halves on a large plate.

5 Using a fork, blend egg yolks with mayonnaise, dressing, salt, pepper, corned beef, and caraway seeds. Fold in cheese. Spoon mixture into egg white halves. Serve.

THOUSAND ISLAND DRESSING VERSUS RUSSIAN DRESSING
Traditionally, Russian dressing (the spicier counterpart to Thousand Island dressing) is served on Reuben sandwiches. Both are pretty similar, so if you prefer Russian to Thousand Island, substitute it in this recipe.

Classic Hot Wings

If you use your air fryer for only one food, make it chicken wings! The convection heat cooks that chicken skin on all sides, making each bite equally crispy on the outside and juicy on the inside.

- **Hands-On Time: 15 minutes**
- **Cook Time: 44 minutes**

Serves 6

1 tablespoon water
2 pounds chicken wings, split at the joint
1 tablespoon butter, room temperature
½ cup buffalo wing sauce

HOW TO SEPARATE CHICKEN WINGS

Some grocery stores will have the wings already broken down for the consumer; however, sometimes you may have to purchase whole wings. To separate, stretch the wing out. Using kitchen shears or a sharp knife, cut the portions at the joints to yield a drumette, wingette, and tip. The tips are not typically used in prepared chicken wings, so you can refrigerate them to use to make broth or season soups.

1 Preheat air fryer at 250°F for 3 minutes.

2 Place water in bottom of air fryer to ensure minimum smoke from fat drippings.

3 Place half of chicken wings in air fryer basket lightly greased with preferred cooking oil. Cook 6 minutes. Flip wings, then cook an additional 6 minutes.

4 While wings are cooking, combine butter and wing sauce in a large bowl.

5 Increase temperature on air fryer to 400°F. Flip wings and cook 5 minutes. Flip once more and cook an additional 5 minutes.

6 Once done, transfer to bowl with sauce and toss. Set aside.

7 Repeat process with remaining wings. Serve warm.

Honey Mustard Wings

These wings are heaven on earth with the addition of the very popular honey mustard flavor. To add a little punch to the sweetness, mix in a little hot sauce or sub in spicy mustard.

- **Hands-On Time:** 15 minutes
- **Cook Time:** 44 minutes

Serves 6

1 tablespoon water
2 pounds chicken wings, split at the joint
1 tablespoon butter, melted
1 tablespoon Dijon mustard
2 tablespoons yellow mustard
¼ cup honey
1 teaspoon apple cider vinegar
⅛ teaspoon salt

1 Preheat air fryer at 250°F for 3 minutes.

2 Place water in bottom of air fryer to ensure minimum smoke from fat drippings.

3 Place half of wings in air fryer basket lightly greased with preferred cooking oil. Cook 6 minutes. Flip wings, then cook an additional 6 minutes.

4 While wings are cooking, combine butter, Dijon mustard, yellow mustard, honey, cider vinegar, and salt in a large bowl.

5 Raise temperature on air fryer to 400°F. Flip wings and cook 5 minutes. Flip wings once more and cook an additional 5 minutes.

6 Transfer cooked wings to bowl with sauce and toss. Repeat process with remaining wings. Serve warm.

Pizza Bombs

Dip these scrumptious little Pizza Bombs in a warmed marinara sauce as an after-school snack or as a quick appetizer on game day. The salty pepperoni and melty mozzarella are a winning combination!

- **Hands-On Time:** 10 minutes
- **Cook Time:** 12 minutes

Yields 9 pizza bites

⅓ cup gluten-free all-purpose flour

¼ teaspoon salt

¼ teaspoon baking powder

½ cup small-diced pepperoni

2 ounces cream cheese, room temperature

¼ cup shredded mozzarella cheese

½ teaspoon Italian seasoning

2 tablespoons whole milk

1 teaspoon olive oil

½ cup marinara sauce, warmed

1 Preheat air fryer at 325°F for 5 minutes.

2 In a small bowl, combine flour, salt, and baking powder.

3 In a medium bowl, combine remaining ingredients, except marinara sauce, mixing until smooth. Add dry ingredients to bowl and mix until well combined.

4 Form mixture into nine (1″) balls and place on ungreased pizza pan. It's fine if pizza balls are touching. Place pan in air fryer basket and cook 12 minutes.

5 Transfer balls to a large plate. Serve warm with marinara sauce on the side for dipping.

Cauliflower Personal Pizza Crusts

There are so many vegetable "rice" options available in the produce section of most grocery stores. Apart from cauliflower rice, you can also find broccoli rice and even a mixture called "confetti rice." Get creative and try these in place of the cauliflower rice in this pizza crust recipe. They work as a perfect substitution, and you may finally be able to get those picky eaters to eat their broccoli!

- **Hands-On Time:** 10 minutes
- **Cook Time:** 30 minutes

Serves 2

1 cup cauliflower rice
1 large egg
½ cup grated mozzarella cheese
1 tablespoon grated Parmesan cheese
1 clove garlic, peeled and minced
1 teaspoon Italian seasoning
⅛ teaspoon salt

1. Preheat air fryer at 400°F for 3 minutes.

2. In a medium bowl, combine all ingredients.

3. Divide mixture in half and spread into two pizza pans lightly greased with preferred cooking oil.

4. Place one pan in air fryer basket and cook 12 minutes. Once done, remove pan from basket and repeat with second pan.

5. Top crusts with your favorite toppings and cook an additional 3 minutes.

CAULIFLOWER RICE

Although pre-made cauliflower rice can be purchased in most grocery stores, it is very easy to make at home. Simply grate the head of one cauliflower bunch using a box grater. You can also place cauliflower florets in a blender with 1 cup of water and blend until desired consistency. Then simply strain out the water and pat the "rice" dry with paper towels.

Retro Party Chex Snack

Some original snack mix recipes include bagel chips, pretzels, and Wheat Chex. But who needs all of that gluten? This recipe is crave-worthy and will take you back in time to the salty-sweet family favorite beloved since the 1970s.

- **Hands-On Time:** 5 minutes
- **Cook Time:** 5 minutes

Serves 4

2 cups Rice Chex
2 cups Corn Chex
¼ cup mixed nuts
¼ teaspoon salt
3 tablespoons butter, melted

1 Preheat air fryer at 350°F for 3 minutes.

2 In a medium bowl, combine all ingredients.

3 Place Chex mixture into ungreased air fryer basket. Cook 3 minutes. Shake basket, then cook an additional 2 minutes.

4 Transfer mixture to a serving bowl. Let cool 5 minutes, then serve warm.

Roasted Pumpkin Seeds

After getting down and dirty with pumpkin guts while carving your jack-o'-lantern, don't forget to save those seeds. The air fryer roasts these gems to perfection, so you can enjoy an antioxidant-rich snack every day of the week!

- **Hands-On Time:** 10 minutes
- **Cook Time:** 13 minutes

Serves 4

2 cups fresh pumpkin seeds, rinsed and dried
2 teaspoons olive oil
½ teaspoon + ¼ teaspoon salt, divided

1 Preheat air fryer at 325°F for 3 minutes.

2 In a medium bowl, toss seeds with oil and ½ teaspoon salt.

3 Place seeds in ungreased air fryer basket. Cook 7 minutes. Using a spatula, turn seeds, then cook an additional 6 minutes.

4 Transfer seeds to a medium bowl and let cool 5 minutes before serving.

Trail Mix Chex Snack

They should put a warning label on this snack mix: it is addictive. It is perfect for munching on while streaming the latest TV series, or taking along during long car trips. You'll also want to pack it in your work lunch or for a picnic! No one will ever know that what they are eating is gluten-free!

- **Hands-On Time:** 5 minutes
- **Cook Time:** 5 minutes

Serves 4

3 cups Rice Chex
¼ cup salted pumpkin seeds
¼ cup crushed pecans
¼ teaspoon ground cinnamon
1 tablespoon light brown sugar
¼ teaspoon salt
3 tablespoons butter, melted
2 tablespoons raisins
2 tablespoons unsweetened coconut flakes
¼ cup mini chocolate chips

1 Preheat air fryer at 350°F for 3 minutes.

2 In a medium bowl, combine Rice Chex, pumpkin seeds, pecans, cinnamon, brown sugar, salt, and butter.

3 Place Rice Chex mixture into ungreased air fryer basket. Cook 3 minutes. Shake basket, then cook an additional 2 minutes.

4 Transfer Rice Chex mixture to a large bowl. Let cool 15 minutes.

5 Once mixture cools, toss in raisins, coconut, and chocolate chips. Serve.

OTHER DRIED FRUITS
Although this recipe calls for raisins, feel free to used diced dried blueberries, pineapple, mango, or cranberries. Whatever your palate desires, dice it up and add it to this flavorful treat!

Grilled Pimento Cheese Croutons

Do you love croutons in a warm bowl of tomato soup? Well, c'mon down South and try these delicious Grilled Pimento Cheese Croutons. You'll never go back to store-bought croutons! And if soup is not on the menu, throw them on a salad or enjoy uncut and grilled with some sliced tomatoes for a tasty sandwich.

- **Hands-On Time:** 10 minutes
- **Cook Time:** 24 minutes

Serves 4

8 ounces shredded sharp Cheddar cheese

1 (4-ounce) jar chopped pimientos, including juice

½ cup mayonnalse

¼ teaspoon salt

¼ teaspoon ground black pepper

8 slices gluten-free sandwich bread

4 tablespoons butter, melted

WHAT ARE PIMIENTOS?
Registering at the lowest level on the Scoville scale of heat, these red, heart-shaped peppers are most commonly stuffed in green olives or used in pimento cheese spread. They are also a nice surprise added to squash fritters or casseroles.

1 Combine cheese, pimientos including juice, mayonnaise, salt, and pepper in a medium bowl. Refrigerate covered 30 minutes.

2 Preheat air fryer at 350°F for 3 minutes.

3 Spread pimento cheese mixture evenly over four slices gluten-free bread. Top each slice with a plain slice and press down just enough to not smoosh cheese out of edges of sandwich.

4 Brush top and bottom of each sandwich lightly with melted butter. Place one sandwich at a time in ungreased air fryer basket and cook 3 minutes. Flip sandwich and cook an additional 3 minutes. Repeat with remaining sandwiches.

5 Slice each sandwich into sixteen sections and serve warm.

Eggplant Parmesan Fries

Making the classic eggplant Parmesan dish can seem a bit daunting and time-consuming, so why not make this easy fry version instead? You'll get all of the flavor with none of the hassle. Plus, self-proclaimed vegetable haters may change their tune once they try this incredibly delicious and crispy snack.

- **Hands-On Time:** 10 minutes
- **Cook Time:** 12 minutes

Serves 2

2 large eggs

2 tablespoons whole milk

½ cup gluten-free bread crumbs

½ cup grated Parmesan cheese

1 teaspoon salt

1 medium eggplant, cut into ½″ rounds, then sliced

½ cup marinara sauce, warmed

1 Preheat air fryer to 400°F for 3 minutes.

2 Whisk together eggs and milk in a medium bowl. In a separate shallow dish, combine bread crumbs, Parmesan cheese, and salt.

3 Dip eggplant in egg mixture. Dredge in bread crumb mixture.

4 Place eggplant fries in ungreased air fryer basket and cook 5 minutes. Flip fries, then cook an additional 5 minutes. Flip once more and cook an additional 2 minutes.

5 Transfer fries to a large plate and serve with warmed marinara sauce on the side for dipping.

First-Rate French Fries

By boiling the potatoes prior to air frying, the fry centers become tender while the exteriors get that nice crunch from the air fryer. There's no need for fast food in order to satisfy that French fry craving when this healthier alternative is so easy to achieve at home.

- **Hands-On Time:** 10 minutes
- **Cook Time:** 15 minutes

Serves 4

2 medium russet potatoes, scrubbed and cut into ¼" fries
3 teaspoons salt, divided

1 Place fries in a medium saucepan. Add water to pan to cover fries. Add 1 teaspoon salt. Bring to a boil over high heat. Boil 3 minutes until fork tender. Drain.

2 Preheat air fryer to 400°F for 3 minutes.

3 Toss fries with 1 teaspoon salt. Place salted fries in ungreased air fryer basket and cook 5 minutes. Shake basket, then cook an additional 5 minutes. Shake basket once more and season with remaining teaspoon salt. Cook an additional 5 minutes.

4 Transfer fries to a large plate and serve warm.

Crispy Zucchini Fries

These breaded zucchini fries are excellent on their own, but are even better dipped in ranch or your own favorite sauce. A healthy alternative to drive-thru French fries, this treat is delicious!

- **Hands-On Time:** 10 minutes
- **Cook Time:** 20 minutes

Serves 2

1 large zucchini, cut into ¼″ fries
1 teaspoon salt
½ cup buttermilk
¾ cup gluten-free bread crumbs
2 teaspoons dried thyme

WHAT ABOUT ITALIAN-STYLE GLUTEN-FREE BREAD CRUMBS?

The two most common gluten-free bread crumbs available commercially are plain and Italian-style. If you have only the Italian-style on hand, simply substitute these for the plain and eliminate the dried thyme.

1 Scatter zucchini fries evenly over a paper towel. Sprinkle with salt. Let sit 10 minutes, then pat with paper towels.

2 Preheat air fryer to 375°F for 3 minutes.

3 Pour buttermilk into a shallow dish. Place bread crumbs in a second shallow dish. Dip zucchini in buttermilk, then dredge in bread crumbs.

4 Place half of zucchini fries in ungreased air fryer basket and cook 5 minutes. Flip fries, then cook an additional 5 minutes.

5 Transfer fries to a large serving dish. Repeat cooking steps with remaining fries. Season with thyme and serve warm.

Dill Pickle Chips

These Alabama delights are perfect served with Sriracha Mayonnaise. The brininess of the pickles, the crispness of the chips, and the creaminess of the sauce will make these a family favorite in no time!

- **Hands-On Time:** 10 minutes
- **Cook Time:** 16 minutes

Serves 4

2 large eggs
¼ cup whole milk
1 teaspoon Worcestershire sauce
½ cup gluten-free bread crumbs
½ cup Bob's Red Mill Gluten Free Cornbread Mix
1 teaspoon garlic powder
1 teaspoon salt
1 (16-ounce) jar dill pickle chips, drained and patted dry

1 Preheat air fryer at 400°F for 3 minutes.

2 Whisk together eggs, milk, and Worcestershire sauce in a small bowl.

3 Combine bread crumbs, cornbread mix, garlic powder, and salt in a shallow dish.

4 Dip pickle slices in egg mixture. Dredge in cornmeal mixture, shaking off any excess.

5 Add half of pickle slices to ungreased air fryer basket and cook 4 minutes. Shake basket and flip pickles. Cook an additional 4 minutes.

6 Transfer cooked chips to a large plate. Repeat with remaining pickles. Serve.

SRIRACHA MAYONNAISE
Delicious, spicy mayonnaise for your Dill Pickle Chips, vegetable fries, tacos, and more is easy! Simply combine ½ cup mayonnaise, 2 teaspoons sriracha, 1 teaspoon lime juice, and ⅛ teaspoon salt in a small bowl. Cover and refrigerate until ready to use, up to one week. Recipe yields ½ cup Sriracha Mayonnaise.

Chili-Corn Chip Avocado Fries

These will become your new, addictive, fantastically awesome snack. Although gluten-free bread crumbs can be used, the crushed chili corn chips are a natural flavor complement to the avocado.

- **Hands-On Time:** 10 minutes
- **Cook Time:** 10 minutes

Serves 2

1 large egg
2 tablespoons whole milk
1 cup crushed chili corn chips
1 medium avocado, halved, peeled, pitted, and sliced into 12 "fries"

1 Preheat air fryer to 375°F for 3 minutes.

2 Whisk together egg and milk in a small bowl. Add chili corn chip crumbs to a separate shallow dish.

3 Dip avocado slices into egg mixture. Dredge in chip crumbs to coat.

4 Place half of avocado slices in air fryer basket lightly greased with preferred cooking oil. Cook 5 minutes. Transfer to serving plate and repeat with remaining avocado slices.

5 Serve fries warm.

Ranch Baby Potato Chips

Everything is cuter in itty-bitty form. By using fingerling potatoes, you're able to achieve this cuteness while pleasing the taste buds of the people eating them.

- **Hands-On Time:** 10 minutes
- **Cook Time:** 16 minutes

Serves 2

1 teaspoon dry ranch seasoning mix
½ teaspoon salt
¼ teaspoon ground black pepper
2 cups thinly sliced scrubbed fingerling potatoes
2 teaspoons olive oil

1 Preheat air fryer to 400°F for 3 minutes.

2 Combine ranch seasoning mix, salt, and pepper in a small bowl. Set aside ½ teaspoon for garnish.

3 Toss sliced potatoes with oil in a medium bowl. Sprinkle with seasoning mix, except reserved ½ teaspoon, to coat.

4 Place chips in ungreased air fryer basket and cook 3 minutes. Shake basket. Cook an additional 3 minutes.

5 Shake basket. Cook 5 minutes. Shake basket once more. Cook an additional 5 minutes.

6 Transfer chips to a medium bowl. Garnish with remaining seasoning, then let rest 15 minutes before serving.

Barbecue Potato Chips

Slicing the potato paper-thin and consistently is the key to perfect potato chips. The air fryer will brown the edges, but be sure to check on them toward the end of the cooking time as they can go from brown to burned quickly!

- **Hands-On Time:** 10 minutes
- **Cook Time:** 17 minutes

Serves 2

½ teaspoon smoked paprika

¼ teaspoon chili powder

¼ teaspoon garlic powder

⅛ teaspoon onion powder

⅛ teaspoon cayenne pepper

⅛ teaspoon light brown sugar

1 teaspoon salt, divided

1 medium russet potato, scrubbed and sliced into ⅛"-thick circles

2 teaspoons olive oil

1 Preheat air fryer to 400°F for 3 minutes.

2 In a large bowl, combine smoked paprika, chili powder, garlic powder, onion powder, cayenne pepper, brown sugar, and ½ teaspoon salt. Set aside.

3 In a separate large bowl, toss chips with olive oil and ½ teaspoon salt.

4 Place chips in ungreased air fryer basket and cook 6 minutes. Shake basket, then cook an additional 5 minutes. Shake basket once more and cook an additional 6 minutes.

5 Transfer chips to bowl with seasoning mix and toss. Let rest 15 minutes before serving.

4

Side Dishes

Sometimes in the attempt to live within the guidelines of a gluten-free diet, you cook up a chicken breast or steak because it is easy, and fall short on the extras and sides because they seem like too much work. All the while the fresh produce you carefully chose at the grocery store or farmers' market takes a back seat in the refrigerator, eventually getting slimy and making it to the trash can instead of your plate. Not only is it a waste of healthful food, but it is also a waste of money. Thankfully, with the air fryer, you can have roasted seasonal vegetables in minutes—all while the main dish is being prepared.

With recipes ranging from Sesame Roasted Carrots and Air-Fried Broccolini to Mexican-Style Twice-Baked Potatoes and Blistered Insalata Caprese, everything you need for easy, delectable sides is included in this chapter. You will be happy you took the few extra moments to prepare a side dish. And your body will thank you too!

Garlic Parmesan Asparagus

Watch the time on this recipe: asparagus can come in very skinny or very thick stalks, so cooking times may vary. This recipe was made with medium-thick stalks. Also, try this dish with white or purple asparagus for a different look and slightly different taste!

- **Hands-On Time:** 5 minutes
- **Cook Time:** 9 minutes

Serves 4

1 pound medium-thick asparagus (about 30 stalks), woody ends discarded

2 teaspoons olive oil

⅛ teaspoon salt

1 clove garlic, peeled and minced

2 tablespoons grated Parmesan cheese

1 Preheat air fryer at 375°F for 3 minutes.

2 In a large bowl, toss asparagus with olive oil.

3 Add asparagus to ungreased air fryer basket and cook 5 minutes. Toss. Cook an additional 4 minutes.

4 Transfer asparagus to a large serving dish and toss with salt, garlic, and Parmesan cheese until coated. Serve warm.

Rainbow Carrots (pictured)

You don't have to be a unicorn to enjoy the beauty and delicious taste of these colorful carrots. Not only are they sweeter, but they are also less earthy in flavor than their deep orange counterparts. This opens the door to those who may *think* they don't enjoy cooked carrots!

- **Hands-On Time: 5 minutes**
- **Cook Time: 11 minutes**

Serves 4

2 pounds rainbow carrots, peeled, greens trimmed and tops removed, cut lengthwise
1 tablespoon butter, melted
½ teaspoon salt

1 Preheat air fryer at 375°F for 3 minutes.

2 In a large bowl, toss carrots with butter and salt.

3 Add carrots to ungreased air fryer basket and cook 5 minutes. Toss, then cook an additional 6 minutes. Serve warm.

Blistered Shishito Peppers

Although these mild peppers can be eaten raw, when you air fry them, they get a little char that makes them taste even better. Add just a touch of sesame oil, and these peppers are a perfect side dish! Switch up the flavor by changing the oil.

- **Hands-On Time: 5 minutes**
- **Cook Time: 8 minutes**

Serves 2

6 ounces shishito peppers (about 3½ cups)
1 teaspoon olive oil
1 teaspoon salt, divided

1 Preheat air fryer at 375°F for 3 minutes.

2 In a medium bowl, toss peppers with oil and ½ teaspoon salt.

3 Add peppers to ungreased air fryer basket and cook 4 minutes. Shake basket. Cook an additional 4 minutes until peppers are blistered.

4 Transfer peppers to a large serving dish and garnish with remaining salt. Serve warm.

Roasted Cajun Okra

Okra can get a bad rap for its slimy texture. This slime, or *mucilage*, is actually edible, and can turn some people away. Choosing smaller pods helps cut out some of this sliminess. In addition, quick-frying the okra makes it taste incredible. This recipe is a great side dish for chicken, steak, or fish!

- **Hands-On Time:** 10 minutes
- **Cook Time:** 7 minutes

Serves 2

2 large eggs
¼ cup whole milk
¼ cup gluten-free bread crumbs
¼ cup cornmeal
1 tablespoon Cajun seasoning
1 teaspoon salt
½ pound fresh okra, sliced into ½" pieces
1 tablespoon butter, melted

1 In a small bowl, whisk together eggs and milk.

2 In a separate shallow dish, combine bread crumbs, cornmeal, Cajun seasoning, and salt.

3 Preheat air fryer at 400°F for 3 minutes.

4 Dip okra in egg mixture. Dredge in bread crumb mixture.

5 Place coated okra in air fryer basket lightly greased with preferred cooking oil. Cook 4 minutes. Shake basket. Brush okra with melted butter. Cook an additional 3 minutes.

6 Transfer cooked okra to a large dish and serve warm.

Buttered Green Beans with Roasted Almonds

Green beans are a go-to side dish for many people, but somehow adding slivered almonds really ups the fancy factor. Not only that, but you are also adding protein and crunch to the dish.

- **Hands-On Time:** 5 minutes
- **Cook Time:** 12 minutes

Serves 4

¼ cup slivered almonds

2 cups fresh green beans, ends trimmed

2 tablespoons butter, melted and divided

½ teaspoon salt

¼ teaspoon ground black pepper

1 Preheat air fryer at 375°F for 3 minutes.

2 Place almonds in ungreased air fryer basket. Cook 1 minute. Toss. Cook an additional minute.

3 Transfer almonds to a small bowl and set aside.

4 In a medium bowl, toss together green beans, 1 tablespoon butter, salt, and pepper.

5 Add green beans to ungreased air fryer basket and cook 5 minutes. Toss. Cook an additional 5 minutes.

6 Transfer green beans to a large serving dish. Serve warm, tossed with remaining butter and garnished with roasted almond slivers.

Air-Fried Broccolini

You may have noticed broccolini showing up more and more in grocery stores as a tasty staple. It is a little sweeter than its larger variety, with smaller stems and leaves and a note of asparagus flavor. Eat it air fried by itself or chopped up in a salad.

- **Hands-On Time:** 10 minutes
- **Cook Time:** 9 minutes

Serves 2

1 bunch broccolini (about ¾ pound), 1" trimmed from stalks
2 tablespoons butter, cubed
¼ teaspoon salt

1 Preheat air fryer at 350°F for 3 minutes.

2 Bring a medium saucepan of salted water to a boil over high heat. Add broccolini and boil 3 minutes.

3 Drain broccolini and transfer to a medium bowl. Toss with butter and salt.

4 Add broccolini to ungreased air fryer basket. Cook 6 minutes.

5 Transfer cooked broccolini to a large serving dish. Serve warm.

Sesame Roasted Carrots

These carrots are super simple to make and have lots of flavor thanks to the richness of the sesame oil. They are a perfect accompaniment to any Asian-seasoned fish or chicken dish.

- **Hands-On Time: 5 minutes**
- **Cook Time:** 10 minutes

Serves 4

3 large carrots, peeled, tops removed, and cut into ½" coins
1 tablespoon sesame oil
½ teaspoon salt

1 Preheat air fryer at 375°F for 3 minutes.

2 In a large bowl, toss carrots with sesame oil. Sprinkle with salt.

3 Add carrots to ungreased air fryer basket and cook 5 minutes. Toss. Cook an additional 5 minutes. Serve warm.

Balsamic Honey Brussels Sprouts

The tart flavor of the balsamic vinegar and the sweetness of the honey help counter the bitter notes that some people detect in Brussels sprouts. This side dish will have your family asking for seconds!

- **Hands-On Time: 5 minutes**
- **Cook Time:** 10 minutes

Serves 4

2 tablespoons balsamic vinegar
1 tablespoon olive oil
1 tablespoon honey
¼ teaspoon salt
⅛ teaspoon ground black pepper
1 pound Brussels sprouts, quartered

1 Preheat air fryer at 350°F for 3 minutes.

2 Whisk together balsamic vinegar, olive oil, honey, salt, and pepper in a large bowl. Toss in Brussels sprouts quarters.

3 Add Brussels sprouts to ungreased air fryer basket. Cook 5 minutes. Toss. Cook an additional 5 minutes.

4 Transfer Brussels sprouts to a large serving dish. Serve warm.

Roasted Acorn Squash

If you are craving some of the side dishes traditionally savored during the holidays, but it is not yet time to celebrate, roast acorn squash. Adding the brown sugar and spices will fill that holiday void long before company arrives!

- **Hands-On Time: 10 minutes**
- **Cook Time: 35 minutes**

Serves 2

½ large acorn squash (from 1 large acorn squash cut in half lengthwise)

1 teaspoon butter, melted

2 teaspoons light brown sugar

⅛ teaspoon ground cinnamon

⅛ teaspoon ground nutmeg

⅛ teaspoon salt

1 Preheat air fryer at 400°F for 3 minutes.

2 Save half of squash for later. Slice off about ¼" from side of remaining squash half to sit flat as a bowl.

3 Combine butter, brown sugar, cinnamon, nutmeg, and salt in a small bowl. Brush over top of squash and pour any remaining mixture in middle of squash.

4 Add acorn squash to ungreased air fryer basket. Cook 35 minutes.

5 Cut cooked squash in half and transfer to two serving plates. Serve warm.

Butternut Squash Purée

Use this purée as a substitute in recipes that call for pumpkin purée, such as pies, muffins, and breads. It is also great in risotto, on a fancy pizza, or even when cutting down on the amount of cheese in a macaroni and cheese dish. You can also add a little brown sugar and a dollop of butter for a tasty mash. Look online for more recipes: this stuff is magic!

- **Hands-On Time: 10 minutes**
- **Cook Time: 25 minutes**

Yields approximately 1 cup

1 small butternut squash (about 1.3 pounds), ends discarded, halved lengthwise, and seeded

1 Preheat air fryer at 400°F for 3 minutes.

2 Add butternut squash to ungreased air fryer basket. Cook 25 minutes.

3 Transfer squash to a cutting board and let rest about 10 minutes until cool enough to handle. Scoop out flesh and add to a food processor. Pulse until smooth.

DON'T THROW AWAY THOSE BUTTERNUT SQUASH SEEDS

These seeds are terrific served on salads, as a garnish on butternut squash soup, or even as a quick snack. Not only are they a good source of protein, but they are also rich in calcium and zinc. To prepare, toss cleaned seeds with 1 teaspoon olive oil and ⅛ teaspoon salt. Add to ungreased air fryer basket and cook 2 minutes. Toss, then cook an additional 2 minutes. Sprinkle with ⅛ teaspoon salt.

Roasted Shallots

Stop hiding those beautiful shallots away, chopped up raw in your dishes. Put a crown on these babies and let them shine! By air frying them, their natural sugars come out, and they are a perfect pairing with a juicy steak or pan-fried pork chop.

- **Hands-On Time:** 10 minutes
- **Cook Time:** 10 minutes

Serves 4

8 medium shallots, peeled
2 teaspoons olive oil
¼ teaspoon salt

1 Preheat air fryer at 400°F for 3 minutes.

2 Toss shallots with olive oil and salt in a medium bowl.

3 Add shallots to ungreased air fryer basket. Cook 10 minutes.

4 Transfer shallots to a medium serving dish and serve warm.

WHAT ARE SHALLOTS?
A shallot is a type of onion and a relative of the chive and leek. The shallot is smaller and a bit sweeter than the white onion. It also grows in bunches, like garlic. Because of its sweet nature, the shallot is an exceptional addition to homemade vinaigrettes. One small onion equals approximately three shallots, so feel free to substitute an onion if that is all you have on hand.

Zucchini Fritters

Fritters are traditionally deep-fried items that you can find at any state fair or seaside bar. But take away the gluten and the oil, and you can still enjoy the great taste of these little guys. Dip them in some Sriracha Mayonnaise (Chapter 3) for a truly flavorful experience!

- **Hands-On Time:** 10 minutes
- **Cook Time:** 22 minutes

Serves 4

2 cups grated zucchini (approximately 1 large)

½ cup crumbled feta cheese

2 tablespoons minced peeled yellow onion

1 tablespoon gluten-free all-purpose flour

1 tablespoon cornmeal

1 tablespoon unsalted butter, melted

1 large egg

2 teaspoons chopped fresh dill

¼ teaspoon salt

½ teaspoon ground black pepper

1 cup plain gluten-free bread crumbs

1 Squeeze grated zucchini between paper towels to remove excess moisture, then transfer to a large bowl. Add cheese, onion, flour, cornmeal, butter, egg, dill, salt, and pepper. Combine.

2 Add bread crumbs to a shallow dish.

3 Preheat air fryer at 350°F for 3 minutes.

4 Form zucchini mixture into twelve balls, approximately 2 tablespoons each. Roll each ball in bread crumbs, covering all sides.

5 Place half of fritters on an ungreased pizza pan. Place pan in air fryer basket and cook 6 minutes. Flip fritters, then cook an additional 5 minutes.

6 Transfer fritters to a large plate. Repeat with remaining fritters. Serve warm.

Corn on the Cob

This is the quickest and tastiest Corn on the Cob you'll ever make or eat! The air fryer is your savior during the colder months when the grill is hiding under cover.

- **Hands-On Time:** 5 minutes
- **Cook Time:** 7 minutes

Serves 4

3 large ears of corn, shucked and halved

2 tablespoons butter, melted

½ teaspoon salt

¼ teaspoon ground black pepper

1 Preheat air fryer at 400°F for 3 minutes.

2 In a large bowl, toss corn in melted butter. Season with salt and pepper.

3 Add corn to ungreased air fryer basket and cook 5 minutes. Turn corn. Cook an additional 2 minutes.

4 Transfer corn to serving plates and serve warm.

Baked Sweet Potatoes

Oooh—sweet potatoes. These sweet little tubers are beloved by many, and the air fryer cooks them up perfectly by creating a crisp exterior and a creamy interior.

- **Hands-On Time:** 10 minutes
- **Cook Time:** 45 minutes

Serves 2

1 pound sweet potatoes (about 2 large), scrubbed and perforated with a fork

2 teaspoons olive oil

½ teaspoon salt

2 tablespoons butter

4 teaspoons light brown sugar

1 Preheat air fryer at 400°F for 3 minutes.

2 Rub olive oil over both potatoes. Season with salt. Place in ungreased air fryer basket.

3 Cook potatoes 30 minutes. Flip, then cook an additional 15 minutes.

4 Set potatoes on a cutting board for approximately 10 minutes until cool enough to handle. Once cooled, slice each potato lengthwise. Press ends of one potato together to open up slice. Repeat with second potato.

5 Garnish each potato with butter and brown sugar. Serve warm.

Roasted Purple Potatoes

Purple potatoes are not just full of antioxidants; they are also pretty and fun! Although this recipe can also be made with red or white potatoes of the same size, why wouldn't you choose the striking purple ones?!

- **Hands-On Time:** 5 minutes
- **Cook Time:** 19 minutes

Serves 4

1 tablespoon olive oil

1 teaspoon Dijon mustard

1 teaspoon lemon juice

2 cloves garlic, peeled and minced

⅛ teaspoon + ¼ teaspoon salt, divided

1 pound small purple potatoes, scrubbed and halved

2 tablespoons butter, melted

⅛ teaspoon ground black pepper

1 tablespoon chopped fresh thyme

1 In a small bowl, whisk together olive oil, mustard, lemon juice, garlic, and ⅛ teaspoon salt. Refrigerate covered until ready to use.

2 Preheat air fryer at 350°F for 3 minutes.

3 In a large bowl, combine potatoes, butter, remaining salt, and pepper.

4 Place potatoes in ungreased air fryer basket. Cook 10 minutes. Toss potatoes. Cook an additional 9 minutes.

5 Transfer potatoes to a large serving bowl and toss with olive oil dressing. Garnish with thyme. Serve warm.

Dill and Sour Cream Mashed Potatoes

The fresh dill and sour cream make these mashed potatoes the perfect accompaniment to a fish or chicken dish. Stir in 2 teaspoons of prepared horseradish and serve alongside a juicy steak!

- **Hands-On Time:** 10 minutes
- **Cook Time:** 14 minutes

Serves 4

1 pound Yukon Gold potatoes (about 2 medium), scrubbed and diced into 1" cubes

2 tablespoons butter, melted

½ teaspoon salt

½ teaspoon ground black pepper

⅛ cup whole milk

¼ cup sour cream

1 tablespoon butter, room temperature

¼ cup chopped fresh dill

1   Preheat air fryer at 350°F for 3 minutes.

2   In a large bowl, toss potatoes with melted butter.

3   Place potatoes in ungreased air fryer basket. Cook 7 minutes. Toss potatoes. Cook an additional 7 minutes.

4   Transfer potatoes to a large dish. Mash together with salt, pepper, half of milk, sour cream, and remaining butter. Slowly add remaining milk until desired consistency is reached. Garnish with dill and serve warm.

CAN I USE YOGURT INSTEAD OF SOUR CREAM?

You can absolutely substitute plain yogurt for the sour cream used in this recipe. Choose whole-milk Greek yogurt for a similar consistency. If you choose regular yogurt, you will need to strain the excess liquid out overnight using a cheesecloth.

Thyme for Baby Red Hasselbacks

Hasselback potatoes will impress your guests because they are beautiful fanned out when cooked, but shhhh: don't tell them that they are supereasy to make! If a baked potato and home fries had a baby, it would be the flavor combination you get in this dish. The melted butter cooks down in the nooks and crannies of the potatoes, creating crisp and tender bites.

- **Hands-On Time:** 15 minutes
- **Cook Time:** 20 minutes

Serves 4

6 baby red potatoes, scrubbed

1 tablespoon olive oil

2 tablespoons butter, melted

1 tablespoon chopped fresh thyme leaves, divided

⅛ teaspoon salt

6 teaspoons sour cream

¼ cup chopped fresh parsley

1 Preheat air fryer at 350°F for 3 minutes.

2 Make slices in the width of each potato about ¼" apart without cutting all the way through potato. Brush sliced potatoes with olive oil, both outside and in between slices.

3 Add potatoes to ungreased air fryer basket. Cook 10 minutes.

4 Brush with melted butter, ensuring butter gets between slices. Sprinkle with half of thyme. Cook an additional 10 minutes.

5 Transfer potatoes to a large serving dish. Season with salt. Add dollop of sour cream to the top of each potato. Garnish with remaining thyme. Sprinkle with parsley. Serve warm.

Mexican-Style Twice-Baked Potatoes

Load these potatoes up for a meal worthy of #TacoTuesday! Full of protein from the black beans, acidity from the mild green chilies, creaminess from the cheese, and love from all of the other ingredients, this is a dish you'll want to make over and over again.

- **Hands-On Time:** 10 minutes
- **Cook Time:** 47 minutes

Serves 4

2 teaspoons olive oil

1 pound russet potatoes (about 2 large), scrubbed and perforated with a fork

2 tablespoons sour cream

1 (4-ounce) can diced green chilies, including juice

⅓ cup finely grated Mexican cheese blend

½ teaspoon chili powder

½ teaspoon + ⅛ teaspoon salt, divided

¼ teaspoon ground black pepper

⅓ cup canned black beans, drained and rinsed

¼ cup shredded iceberg lettuce

4 grape tomatoes, sliced

¼ cup chopped fresh cilantro

1 Preheat air fryer at 400°F for 3 minutes.

2 Rub olive oil over both potatoes. Place in ungreased air fryer basket.

3 Cook potatoes 30 minutes. Flip, then cook an additional 15 minutes.

4 Transfer potatoes to a cutting board 10 minutes until cool enough to handle. Once cooled, slice each potato lengthwise. Scoop out all but a ¼" layer of potato to form four "boats."

5 Place scooped-out potato in a medium bowl. Add sour cream, green chilies, cheese, chili powder, ½ teaspoon salt, and black pepper. Mash until smooth. Fold in black beans. Evenly distribute mixture into potato skin boats.

6 Place boats back into air fryer basket and cook an additional 2 minutes.

7 Transfer boats to a large serving plate and garnish with lettuce, tomatoes, and fresh cilantro. Sprinkle tops with remaining salt. Serve warm.

Hammy Potatoes Au Gratin

Although you can serve this for four as a side dish, you can also serve it as a main course for two alongside a side salad as a hearty meal for you and the one you love.

- **Hands-On Time:** 15 minutes
- **Cook Time:** 20 minutes

Serves 4

½ cup half-and-half

2 large eggs

1 tablespoon gluten-free all-purpose flour

1 teaspoon salt

1 teaspoon ground black pepper

1 teaspoon smoked paprika

2 medium russet potatoes, scrubbed and thinly sliced

1 cup diced cooked ham

½ cup grated Gruyère cheese

1 tablespoon butter, melted

1 tablespoon grated Parmesan cheese

1 tablespoon gluten-free plain panko bread crumbs

1 tablespoon fresh thyme leaves

1 In a medium bowl, whisk together half-and-half, eggs, flour, salt, pepper, and smoked paprika. Add potatoes and toss, ensuring all sides of potato slices are coated.

2 Preheat air fryer at 375°F for 3 minutes.

3 Lightly grease a 7″ round cake pan with preferred cooking oil. Evenly distribute half of potato slices in pan. Pour half of egg mixture over potatoes. Layer half of ham and Gruyère cheese on top. Repeat with remaining potato, egg mixture, ham, and Gruyère.

4 In a small bowl, combine butter, Parmesan cheese, bread crumbs, and thyme leaves. Distribute over casserole. Cover pan with aluminum foil.

5 Place pan in air fryer basket. Cook 15 minutes. Remove foil and cook an additional 5 minutes.

6 Remove pan from air fryer and let rest 10 minutes. Serve warm.

Blistered Insalata Caprese

Sometimes classics are considered classics for a reason, so why mess with garden tomatoes, fresh mozzarella, olive oil, and balsamic vinegar topped with basil? Well, blistering the tomatoes brings out their natural sugars even more, lending another delicious note to this fantastic Italian salad. Try it—what do you have to lose?

- **Hands-On Time:** 5 minutes
- **Cook Time:** 15 minutes

Serves 2

4 ounces grape tomatoes (approximately 16)

2 teaspoons olive oil, divided

¼ teaspoon salt

1 (8-ounce) ball mozzarella cheese, sliced

1 tablespoon balsamic vinegar

1 tablespoon chopped fresh basil

¼ teaspoon ground black pepper

1 Preheat air fryer at 350°F for 3 minutes.

2 In a small bowl, toss tomatoes with 1 teaspoon olive oil and salt.

3 Transfer tomatoes to ungreased air fryer basket and cook 5 minutes. Shake basket. Cook 5 minutes. Shake basket once more. Cook an additional 5 minutes.

4 Arrange mozzarella on two serving plates. Add blistered tomatoes on top. Drizzle remaining oil and balsamic vinegar over tomatoes. Garnish with basil and black pepper.

Four Cheese Macaroni and Cheese

Who said that macaroni and cheese wasn't awesome when made gluten-free?! Dare any skeptic to tell the difference in this recipe.

- **Hands-On Time: 15 minutes**
- **Cook Time: 19 minutes**

Serves 4

3 tablespoons butter, divided

1 large sweet yellow onion, peeled and diced

1 tablespoon gluten-free all-purpose flour

4 ounces cream cheese, room temperature

¼ cup shredded Swiss cheese

¼ cup shredded sharp Cheddar cheese

¼ cup grated Parmesan cheese

¼ cup whole milk

½ pound dry gluten-free elbow macaroni, cooked according to package instructions, drained

¼ cup gluten-free bread crumbs

1 In a large skillet over medium-high heat, heat 2 tablespoons butter 30 seconds. Add onion and cook until onions are translucent, about 3 minutes. Whisk in flour until sauce thickens.

2 Add cream cheese, Swiss cheese, Cheddar cheese, Parmesan cheese, and milk to skillet. Stir. Add pasta and toss.

3 Preheat air fryer at 375°F for 3 minutes.

4 In a small bowl, mix together bread crumbs and remaining butter.

5 Spoon pasta mixture into a 7" round cake barrel lightly greased with preferred cooking oil. Top with buttered bread crumbs.

6 Place pan in air fryer basket and cook 15 minutes.

7 Remove pan from air fryer and let rest 10 minutes. Serve warm.

Air-Fried Watermelon Salad

The sugar in the watermelon is brought to life in the air fryer, and when you add the heated melon to the salad, it slightly wilts the arugula and melts the goat cheese. It completely changes the nature of this beautiful salad!

- **Hands-On Time:** 10 minutes
- **Cook Time:** 4 minutes

Serves 4

4 cups (½" cubes) watermelon

½ medium red onion, peeled and sliced into half-moons

4 teaspoons olive oil, divided

½ teaspoon salt

¼ teaspoon ground black pepper

3 cups arugula

1 teaspoon balsamic vinegar

1 teaspoon honey

2 tablespoons crumbled goat cheese

1 tablespoon chopped fresh mint

1 Preheat air fryer at 375°F for 3 minutes.

2 In a large bowl, toss watermelon and onion in 2 teaspoons olive oil. Season with salt and pepper.

3 Add watermelon mixture to ungreased air fryer basket. Cook 2 minutes. Toss, then cook an additional 2 minutes.

4 In a large bowl, add arugula, remaining olive oil, balsamic vinegar, and honey. Toss to coat arugula.

5 Add watermelon and onion to arugula mixture. Garnish with goat cheese and mint. Serve warm.

OTHER AIR-FRIED FRUITS

Air frying fruits brings out more of their natural sugars. Try frying pineapple, peaches, and other melons. Serve as is, or chop them up into fruit salsas and salads.

Bacon and Cheese Rotini Bake

Pasta, bacon, cheese: this is the holy trinity in many households. The decadence of this dish will have your guests coming back for more and more!

- **Hands-On Time: 15 minutes**
- **Cook Time: 19 minutes**

Serves 4

3 tablespoons butter, divided

1 tablespoon gluten-free all-purpose flour

2 ounces cream cheese, room temperature

½ cup shredded sharp Cheddar cheese

½ cup shredded mozzarella cheese

¼ cup heavy cream

½ pound dry gluten-free rotini, cooked according to package instructions, drained

4 pieces cooked bacon, crumbled

¼ cup gluten-free bread crumbs

1 In a large skillet over medium-high heat, heat 2 tablespoons butter 30 seconds. Whisk in flour until sauce thickens.

2 Add cream cheese, Cheddar cheese, mozzarella cheese, and heavy cream to skillet and cook 2 minutes until creamy. Add pasta and bacon and toss to coat.

3 Preheat air fryer at 375°F for 3 minutes.

4 In a small microwave-safe bowl, cook remaining butter in microwave in 10-second intervals until melted, then mix in bread crumbs.

5 Spoon pasta mixture into a 7" round cake barrel lightly greased with preferred cooking oil. Top with buttered bread crumbs.

6 Place pan in air fryer basket and cook 15 minutes.

7 Remove pan from air fryer and let rest 10 minutes. Serve warm.

5

Chicken Main Dishes

This chapter covers one of the most consumed proteins in the United States: chicken. Living a gluten-free life can be lonely sometimes when your options feel limited. But you don't have to miss out on that fried chicken with biscuits on the side! Simply say hello to your new best friend, the air fryer. With the air fryer, you can fry up chicken with a favorite gluten-free breading and enjoy it with gluten-free Buttermilk Biscuits (Chapter 2) in no time. You will also use a significantly lower amount of oil in the preparation. And because of the quicker cooking time, more nutrients stay intact in the air fryer, guaranteeing that your chicken dishes are juicy, delicious, *and* nutritious.

Whether you're craving Herbed Chicken Legs or Green Chile Chicken Quesadillas, or your family is calling for Southern Breaded Drumettes or Buffalo Chicken Patties, you'll find new favorite recipes here!

Prep Day Chicken

Sometimes being prepared for the week is half the battle when trying to watch your waistline, stay within a budget, or cut down on time in the kitchen after a long day. Make these chicken breasts and add them to salads and hearty soups during the week, or heat them up to enjoy as is!

- **Hands-On Time: 5 minutes**
- **Cook Time: 9 minutes**

Serves 4

2 teaspoons olive oil
4 (4-ounce) boneless, skinless chicken breasts (approximately 1 pound)
½ teaspoon salt
¼ teaspoon ground black pepper

1   Preheat air fryer at 350°F for 3 minutes.

2   Brush oil lightly over chicken. Season with salt and pepper.

3   Add chicken to ungreased air fryer basket and cook 4 minutes. Shake basket gently and flip chicken. Cook an additional 5 minutes. Check chicken using a meat thermometer to ensure internal temperature is at least 165°F.

4   Transfer chicken to a large serving plate and let rest 5 minutes. Chop and refrigerate covered up to one week.

Two-Ingredient Salsa Verde Chicken

This is absolutely the easiest, tastiest, and lowest-calorie meal you can prepare in minutes. Serve it topped with extra salsa verde!

- **Hands-On Time: 5 minutes**
- **Cook Time: 30 minutes**

Serves 4

4 (4-ounce) boneless, skinless chicken thighs (approximately 1 pound)
1 cup salsa verde

1   Preheat air fryer at 350°F for 3 minutes.

2   Place chicken thighs in an ungreased 7" square cake barrel. Cover with salsa verde.

3   Place pan in air fryer basket and cook 30 minutes. Use a meat thermometer to ensure internal temperature is at least 165°F.

4   Transfer cooked chicken to a large serving plate and let rest 5 minutes. Serve warm.

Chicken Bulgogi with Rice and Quick Pickled Carrots

Traditionally, bulgogi is a Korean barbecue of marinated beef or pork; however, the dark meat of chicken thighs is also a great venue for the delicious sauce. Coupled with the tameness of the rice and the tanginess of the Quick Pickled Carrots, this chicken makes a perfect meal.

- **Hands-On Time:** 15 minutes
- **Cook Time:** 11 minutes

Serves 4

For Quick Pickled Carrots
2 medium carrots, grated
¼ cup rice vinegar
2 teaspoons granulated sugar
⅛ teaspoon salt

For Chicken and Bulgogi Sauce
2 tablespoons tamari
2 teaspoons sesame oil
1 tablespoon light brown sugar
1 tablespoon rice vinegar
1 tablespoon lime juice
2 cloves garlic, peeled and minced
2 teaspoons minced fresh ginger
3 scallions, sliced, whites and green separated
6 (4-ounce) boneless, skinless chicken thighs (approximately 1½ pounds), cut into 1" cubes
4 cups cooked white rice
2 teaspoons sesame seeds

1 **To make Quick Pickled Carrots:** Combine Quick Pickled Carrots ingredients in a medium bowl. Refrigerate covered until ready to serve.

2 **To make Chicken and Bulgogi Sauce:** In a large bowl, whisk together tamari, sesame oil, brown sugar, rice vinegar, lime juice, garlic, ginger, and whites of scallions. Add chicken thighs and let marinate 10 minutes.

3 Preheat air fryer at 350°F for 3 minutes.

4 Using a slotted spoon, place chicken in ungreased air fryer basket. Set aside remaining marinade.

5 Cook chicken 6 minutes. Shake basket and pour remaining marinade over chicken. Cook an additional 5 minutes. Use a meat thermometer to ensure internal temperature is at least 165°F.

6 Remove chicken from air fryer and place over rice on serving plates. Garnish with scallion greens and sesame seeds. Serve with Quick Pickled Carrots on the side.

Southern Breaded Drumettes

The drumette is the portion of the chicken wing that looks like a smaller chicken leg. Fry these little drumettes up after soaking or brining them in buttermilk for a down South experience on a cuter level!

- **Hands-On Time:** 10 minutes
- **Cook Time:** 20 minutes

Serves 2

1 pound chicken drumettes
1 cup buttermilk
¾ cup gluten-free bread crumbs
½ teaspoon smoked paprika
½ teaspoon garlic powder
½ teaspoon salt

1 In a medium bowl, toss drumettes in buttermilk. Refrigerate covered overnight.

2 Preheat air fryer at 350°F for 3 minutes.

3 Combine bread crumbs, paprika, garlic powder, and salt in a shallow dish. Shake excess buttermilk off drumettes and dredge in bread crumb mixture.

4 Add chicken to air fryer basket lightly greased with preferred cooking oil and cook 12 minutes.

5 Increase air fryer temperature to 400°F. Gently flip chicken and cook 4 minutes. Flip chicken once more. Cook an additional 4 minutes. Use a meat thermometer to ensure internal temperature is at least 165°F.

6 Transfer chicken to a large serving plate and let rest 5 minutes. Serve warm.

Herbed Chicken Legs

Prep these chicken legs the night before, and in a little over 30 minutes the next night you'll be serving up a tasty meal. While the legs are cooking, put together a fresh salad or just go watch an episode of your current favorite show. The legs will be done in no time!

- **Hands-On Time: 10 minutes**
- **Cook Time: 36 minutes**

Serves 4

1 cup plain Greek yogurt

1 tablespoon Dijon mustard

1 teaspoon smoked paprika

1 teaspoon garlic powder

1 teaspoon dried oregano

1 teaspoon dried thyme

⅛ teaspoon ground nutmeg

1 teaspoon salt

1 teaspoon ground black pepper

6 (4-ounce) chicken legs (approximately 1½ pounds)

3 tablespoons butter, melted

1 In a medium bowl, combine yogurt, Dijon mustard, smoked paprika, garlic powder, dried oregano, dried thyme, nutmeg, salt, and pepper. Add chicken and toss until coated. Refrigerate covered 60 minutes up to overnight.

2 Preheat air fryer at 375°F for 3 minutes.

3 Shake excess marinade from chicken. Add half of chicken to air fryer basket lightly greased with preferred cooking oil and cook 10 minutes.

4 Brush chicken lightly with melted butter. Flip and brush other side with butter. Cook an additional 8 minutes. Use a meat thermometer to ensure internal temperature is at least 165°F.

5 Transfer chicken to a large serving plate and let rest 5 minutes. Repeat process with remaining chicken. Serve warm.

Greek "Grilled" Chicken Salad

If you are making this as a side salad for dinner and have leftovers, wrap them up in a gluten-free tortilla for a very tasty lunch the next day.

- **Hands-On Time:** 10 minutes
- **Cook Time:** 10 minutes

Serves 2

For Dressing

1 cup plain Greek yogurt
½ medium English cucumber, peeled and small-diced
1 teaspoon chopped fresh dill
1 teaspoon chopped fresh mint
½ teaspoon salt
1 teaspoon lemon juice
2 cloves garlic, peeled and minced

For Chicken

1 pound boneless, skinless chicken cutlets, cut into ⅓"-thick strips
½ teaspoon salt
¼ teaspoon ground black pepper

For Salad

3 cups mixed greens
¼ cup diced peeled red onion
10 kalamata olives, pitted and halved
1 large Roma tomato, diced
¼ cup feta cheese crumbles

1 Preheat air fryer at 350°F for 3 minutes.

2 **To make Dressing:** Combine Dressing ingredients in a small bowl. Cover and keep refrigerated until ready to use (up to one week).

3 **To make Chicken:** Place chicken in medium bowl. Season with salt and pepper.

4 Add chicken strips to air fryer basket lightly greased with preferred cooking oil. Cook 5 minutes. Toss gently, then cook an additional 5 minutes. Check with a meat thermometer to ensure internal temperature is at least 165°F.

5 **To make Salad:** Add mixed greens to two medium salad bowls. Garnish with onions, olives, tomatoes, and feta cheese. Top with chicken and drizzle with Dressing. Serve.

Korean Barbecue Chicken Legs

Move over sriracha; gochujang is here and taking over the culinary world. A fermented chili paste, this earthy condiment is not quite as spicy as sriracha, and has a sweet and tangy component like ketchup. Slather it on chicken legs with a few other spices and it will help create the best chicken you make this year!

- **Hands-On Time:** 10 minutes
- **Cook Time:** 36 minutes

Serves 4

4 scallions, sliced, whites and greens separated
¼ cup tamari
2 tablespoons sesame oil
¼ cup honey
2 tablespoons gochujang
4 cloves garlic, peeled and minced
½ teaspoon ground ginger
1 teaspoon salt
½ teaspoon ground white pepper
6 (4-ounce) chicken legs (approximately 1½ pounds)

WHAT IS TAMARI?
Tamari is a gluten-free soy sauce substitute and is a by-product of miso. The flavor is a bit more robust than soy sauce but is excellent for 1:1 substitution in recipes calling for soy sauce.

1. Mince whites of scallions. Set aside greens. In a medium bowl, combine tamari, sesame oil, honey, gochujang, garlic, ginger, salt, pepper, and whites of scallions. Set aside ¼ cup marinade. Add chicken legs to bowl. Refrigerate covered 30 minutes.

2. Preheat air fryer at 350°F for 3 minutes.

3. Add half of chicken to air fryer basket lightly greased with preferred cooking oil and cook 10 minutes. Flip chicken.

4. Increase air fryer temperature to 400°F. Cook 8 minutes. Use a meat thermometer to ensure internal temperature is at least 165°F.

5. Transfer chicken to a large serving dish and let rest 5 minutes. Repeat with remaining chicken. Toss cooked chicken with remaining sauce, garnish with sliced scallion greens, and serve warm.

Buffalo Chicken Patties

Ground chicken can tend to be a little bland and dry when cooked. The addition of the carrot and celery lends a moistness to these patties, and the wing sauce is always a flavor favorite. If you don't like blue cheese with your buffalo sauce, you can substitute both the blue cheese and sour cream with ranch dressing for your sauce.

- **Hands-On Time:** 10 minutes
- **Cook Time:** 26 minutes

Serves 4

¼ cup crumbled blue cheese

¼ cup sour cream

⅛ teaspoon salt

3 tablespoons buffalo wing sauce, divided

1 pound ground chicken

2 tablespoons finely grated carrot

2 tablespoons finely diced celery

1 large egg white

1 In a small bowl, combine blue cheese, sour cream, salt, and 1 tablespoon buffalo wing sauce. Refrigerate covered until ready to serve patties.

2 Preheat air fryer at 350°F for 3 minutes.

3 In a large bowl, combine remaining buffalo sauce, chicken, carrot, celery, and egg white. Form mixture into four patties, making a slight indentation in middle of each.

4 Add two patties to air fryer basket lightly greased with preferred cooking oil and cook 6 minutes. Flip patties and cook an additional 7 minutes until desired doneness.

5 Transfer patties to a large serving plate. Repeat cooking steps with remaining patties. Serve with blue cheese sauce.

Chicken Satay Kebabs with Peanut Sauce

If you don't have a kebab set, use short wooden skewers that have been soaked in water for at least 30 minutes. Also, rotate the skewers twice during the cooking process. Enjoy dipping the chicken in this easy-to-make Peanut Sauce.

- **Hands-On Time:** 10 minutes
- **Cook Time:** 24 minutes

Serves 4

For Peanut Sauce
¼ cup creamy peanut butter

1 tablespoon pure maple syrup

1 tablespoon tamari

1 tablespoon lime juice

¼ teaspoon sriracha

2 teaspoons finely chopped peeled yellow onion

¼ teaspoon minced fresh ginger

1 clove garlic, peeled and minced

2 tablespoons water

For Marinade
1 cup coconut milk

1 tablespoon Peanut Sauce

1 teaspoon sriracha

1 tablespoon chopped fresh cilantro

2 (8-ounce) boneless, skinless chicken breasts (about 1 pound), cut into 8 (1"-thick) strips

1 **To make Peanut Sauce:** In a small bowl, whisk together Peanut Sauce ingredients. Reserve 1 tablespoon. Set aside.

2 **To make Marinade:** In a medium bowl, combine coconut milk, reserved Peanut Sauce, sriracha, and cilantro. Toss chicken in. Refrigerate covered 15 minutes.

3 Preheat air fryer at 350°F for 3 minutes.

4 Skewer chicken and place half of skewers on kebab rack. Place kebab rack in air fryer basket. Cook 12 minutes.

5 Transfer cooked kebabs to a large serving dish. Repeat cooking steps with remaining kebabs. Serve warm with Peanut Sauce on the side.

Curried Chicken Salad

Although you can cook up some fresh chicken, this is an excellent meal for utilizing leftover rotisserie chicken. Quick and fruity, creamy and crunchy, this tasty salad is delicious served as a lettuce wrap or with a drizzle of honey on top.

- **Hands-On Time:** 10 minutes
- **Cook Time:** 18 minutes

Serves 2

2 (8-ounce) boneless, skinless chicken breasts (approximately 1 pound)

1 teaspoon salt

¼ teaspoon ground black pepper

¾ cup mayonnaise

1 tablespoon fresh lime juice

1 teaspoon curry powder

⅓ cup chopped golden raisins

1 small Granny Smith apple, peeled, cored, and grated

1 medium scallion, minced

2 tablespoons chopped pecans

1 Preheat air fryer at 350°F for 3 minutes.

2 Season chicken with salt and pepper.

3 Add half of chicken to air fryer basket lightly greased with preferred cooking oil. Cook 4 minutes. Shake basket gently and flip chicken. Cook an additional 5 minutes. Use a meat thermometer to ensure internal temperature is at least 165°F.

4 Transfer chicken to a large plate. Repeat with remaining chicken. Let rest 7 minutes until cool enough to handle.

5 Chop chicken and toss into a large bowl with remaining ingredients. Refrigerate covered until ready to eat.

Air-Fried Chicken Club Sandwiches

Hot out of the air fryer and straight onto the bun, the chicken is the star of this recipe. So, enjoy as is, add a few pickle slices, or mix things up with your own favorite sandwich toppings. The great thing about homemade sandwiches is that each family member can personalize their meal!

- **Hands-On Time:** 10 minutes
- **Cook Time:** 36 minutes

Serves 4

1 cup buttermilk
1 large egg
1 cup gluten-free plain bread crumbs
1 teaspoon garlic powder
1 teaspoon salt
1 teaspoon ground black pepper
4 chicken cutlets (about 2 pounds)
3 tablespoons butter, melted
4 gluten-free hamburger buns
4 tablespoons mayonnaise
4 teaspoons yellow mustard
8 dill pickle chips
4 pieces iceberg lettuce
4 slices cooked bacon
8 thin slices vine-ripe tomato

1 Preheat air fryer at 350°F for 3 minutes.

2 In a medium bowl, whisk together buttermilk and egg.

3 In a separate shallow dish, combine bread crumbs, garlic powder, salt, and black pepper.

4 Dip chicken in buttermilk mixture, then dredge in bread crumb mixture. Shake off any excess crumb mixture.

5 Add two chicken cutlets to air fryer basket lightly greased with preferred cooking oil. Cook 10 minutes.

6 Brush chicken lightly with melted butter on both sides. Increase temperature to 400°F and cook an additional 8 minutes.

7 Use a meat thermometer to check internal temperature of chicken is at least 165°F. Once done, transfer to a large serving plate and let rest 5 minutes. Repeat cooking process with remaining chicken.

8 Assemble sandwiches by spreading mayonnaise on top buns and mustard on bottom buns. Place chicken on bottom buns. Top with pickles, lettuce, bacon, and tomatoes. Serve warm.

Crispy Chicken Cobb Salad

You don't have to go to a restaurant to enjoy a fancy salad. The fresh ingredients create a healthy meal, while the air fryer allows you to enjoy that crispy breaded chicken usually only achieved by deep-frying.

- **Hands-On Time:** 10 minutes
- **Cook Time:** 18 minutes

Serves 2

For Chicken
1 large egg
1 tablespoon honey
1 tablespoon Dijon mustard
½ teaspoon apple cider vinegar
2 (4-ounce) boneless, skinless chicken breasts (approximately ½ pound), cut into 1" cubes
¾ cup plain gluten-free bread crumbs
½ teaspoon salt
½ teaspoon ground black pepper

For Salad
3 cups chopped iceberg lettuce
½ cup ranch dressing
½ medium avocado, peeled, pitted, and diced
1 medium beefsteak tomato, diced
1 large hard-boiled egg, diced
4 slices cooked bacon, crumbled
¼ cup diced peeled red onion

1 **To make Chicken:** Preheat air fryer at 350°F for 3 minutes.

2 In a medium bowl, whisk together egg, honey, Dijon mustard, and vinegar. Toss in chicken cubes.

3 In a shallow dish, combine bread crumbs, salt, and pepper. Shake excess marinade off chicken and dredge in bread crumb mixture.

4 Add half of chicken to air fryer basket lightly greased with preferred cooking oil. Cook 4 minutes. Shake basket gently. Cook an additional 5 minutes. Use a meat thermometer to ensure internal temperature is at least 165°F.

5 Transfer chicken to a plate large plate. Repeat cooking process with remaining chicken.

6 **To make Salad:** Toss lettuce and ranch dressing in two serving bowls. Top with avocado, tomato, egg, bacon, onion, and chicken. Serve.

Chicken Avocado Paninis

Traditionally, paninis go through a special press to toast the bread and melt the cheese. Achieve this toasty, melted goodness with the air fryer, and then give it a gentle press with the back of a skillet to enjoy your homemade paninis!

- **Hands-On Time:** 10 minutes
- **Cook Time:** 12 minutes

Serves 2

2 tablespoons mayonnaise

4 teaspoons yellow mustard

4 slices gluten-free sandwich bread

4 ounces thinly sliced deli chicken

4 ounces thinly sliced provolone cheese

1 small avocado, peeled, pitted, and thinly sliced

1 medium Roma tomato, thinly sliced

¼ teaspoon salt

¼ teaspoon ground black pepper

2 tablespoons butter, melted

1 Preheat air fryer at 350°F for 3 minutes.

2 Spread mayonnaise and mustard on inside of each bread slice. Build sandwiches by evenly distributing chicken, provolone, avocado, and tomato on slices. Sprinkle tomato with salt and pepper, then close sandwiches.

3 Brush top and bottom of each sandwich lightly with melted butter. Place one sandwich in ungreased air fryer basket and cook 3 minutes. Flip and cook an additional 3 minutes. Repeat with remaining sandwich.

4 Transfer sandwiches to serving plates and press gently with back of a skillet. Serve warm.

Ketchup Chicken Strips

Yes, these are a thing! So, if you are a ketchup person rather than a mustard person, these may be your new favorite snack or lunch! Kick things up a little more if you wish with Sriracha Mayonnaise dipping sauce (Chapter 3).

- **Hands-On Time:** 10 minutes
- **Cook Time:** 10 minutes

Serves 2

1 pound boneless, skinless chicken cutlets, cut into ⅓"-thick strips
1 cup ketchup
½ cup plain gluten-free bread crumbs
½ cup cornmeal

1 Place chicken strips in a medium bowl. Add ketchup and toss chicken until fully coated.

2 Preheat air fryer at 350°F for 3 minutes.

3 Combine bread crumbs and cornmeal in a shallow dish. Shake off excess ketchup from chicken strips and dredge in bread crumb mixture. Shake off any excess.

4 Add chicken strips to air fryer basket lightly greased with preferred cooking oil. Cook 4 minutes. Toss chicken gently. Cook an additional 4 minutes. Toss chicken gently once more. Cook 2 more minutes. Use a meat thermometer to ensure internal temperature is at least 165°F.

5 Transfer chicken to a large plate and serve warm.

Horseradish Mustard Chicken Bites

These three-ingredient chicken bites are excellent on salads, atop bowls of rice, or as a tasty side dish. Because the chicken is cut into bite-sized pieces, the cooking time is drastically reduced, cutting down your time in the kitchen.

- **Hands-On Time:** 10 minutes
- **Cook Time:** 9 minutes

Serves 4

2 tablespoons horseradish mustard
1 tablespoon olive oil
2 (8-ounce) boneless, skinless chicken breasts (approximately 1 pound), cut into 1" cubes

HORSERADISH MUSTARD SUBSTITUTIONS

Horseradish mustard lends a distinct spiciness compared to its mild yellow mustard counterpart. If heat isn't your thing, swap it out for any mustard you prefer. There are a myriad of mustard flavors in the condiment aisle of most grocery stores, any of which would be perfect for this recipe. From honey mustard to beer mustard, give 'em all a try!

1. In a medium bowl, whisk together horseradish mustard and olive oil. Add chicken cubes and toss. Refrigerate covered 30 minutes up to overnight.

2. Preheat air fryer at 350°F for 3 minutes.

3. Add chicken to air fryer basket lightly greased with preferred cooking oil. Cook 4 minutes. Toss chicken gently. Cook an additional 5 minutes. Use a meat thermometer to ensure internal temperature is at least 165°F.

4. Transfer chicken bites to a large plate and serve warm.

Chicken Parmesan Pizzadillas

Pizza + Quesadilla = Pizzadilla! This recipe is a great use of that Prep Day Chicken (see recipe in this chapter) you make at the beginning of the week. Get all of the awesome flavors of chicken Parmesan, with some added mozzarella for gooey, cheesy goodness! You can also add a side of extra marinara sauce for dipping.

- **Hands-On Time:** 10 minutes
- **Cook Time:** 12 minutes

Serves 4

2 cups cooked boneless, skinless chicken, shredded

½ teaspoon salt

1 teaspoon garlic powder

3 tablespoons butter, melted

8 (6") gluten-free flour tortillas

1 cup marinara sauce

1 cup grated mozzarella cheese

1 cup grated provolone cheese

8 large fresh basil leaves, julienned

1 Preheat air fryer to 350°F for 3 minutes.

2 In a medium bowl, toss chicken with salt and garlic powder.

3 Lightly brush melted butter on one side of a tortilla. Place tortilla butter side down in ungreased air fryer basket. Spread ¼ cup marinara sauce on tortilla. Layer ½ cup chicken, ¼ cup mozzarella, ¼ cup provolone, and one-quarter basil leaves on top. Top with second tortilla. Lightly butter top of tortilla.

4 Cook pizzadilla 3 minutes. Set aside and repeat with remaining ingredients (yields four pizzadillas total).

5 Slice each pizzadilla into six sections. Serve warm.

FRESH HERBS CAN BE EXPENSIVE

Fresh herbs can add so much flavor to a dish, but sometimes they are just too expensive. Luckily, they are easy to grow at home! If you can, grow them indoors to avoid hassle during the colder months. There are many varieties of indoor herb gardens, from in-pot to contained hanging plants.

Lemony Herb Chicken Meatballs

Whether you are planning to serve these meatballs with rice, tossed into a sauce, or on a meatball sub with gluten-free bread, you won't be disappointed. This is a low-calorie recipe full of flavor!

- **Hands-On Time:** 10 minutes
- **Cook Time:** 16 minutes

Yields 18 meatballs

1 pound ground chicken
1 large egg
¾ cup gluten-free bread crumbs
¼ cup finely diced peeled yellow onion
1 teaspoon Italian seasoning
2 teaspoons lemon zest
1 teaspoon salt
½ teaspoon ground black pepper
¼ cup chopped fresh parsley

1 Preheat air fryer at 350°F for 3 minutes.

2 Combine chicken, egg, bread crumbs, onion, Italian seasoning, lemon zest, salt, and pepper in a large bowl. Form mixture into eighteen meatballs, about 2 tablespoons each.

3 Add nine meatballs to ungreased air fryer basket and cook 6 minutes. Flip meatballs. Cook an additional 2 minutes.

4 Transfer cooked meatballs to serving dish. Repeat with remaining meatballs and garnish with chopped parsley. Serve warm.

Breaded Jalapeño Popper Chicken Meatballs

By pickling the jalapeños, a bit of the zing from the heat is taken away, still leaving them a little spicy—as well as with a touch of sourness.

- **Hands-On Time:** 10 minutes
- **Cook Time:** 10 minutes

Yields 8 meatballs

For Quick Pickled Jalapeños
2 medium jalapeños, seeded and small-diced
2 tablespoons white wine vinegar
½ teaspoon granulated sugar
⅛ teaspoon salt

For Cheese Center
1 tablespoon cream cheese
2 tablespoons shredded Cheddar cheese
1 teaspoon Quick Pickled Jalapeños

For Chicken Meatballs
¾ pound ground chicken
Remaining Quick Pickled Jalapeños
¼ teaspoon smoked paprika
¼ teaspoon salt

For Breading
1 cup gluten-free bread crumbs
¼ teaspoon salt
1 tablespoon butter, melted

1 **To make Quick Pickled Jalapeños:** In a small bowl, combine diced jalapeños, white wine vinegar, sugar, and salt. Refrigerate 15 minutes.

2 **To make Cheese Center:** In a small bowl, combine cream cheese, Cheddar cheese, and 1 teaspoon refrigerated Quick Pickled Jalapeños. Form mixture into eight balls.

3 **To make Chicken Meatballs:** In a medium bowl, combine ground chicken, remaining refrigerated Quick Pickled Jalapeños, smoked paprika, and salt. Form mixture into eight meatballs.

4 Form a hole in one chicken meatball. Press a cheese ball into hole and form chicken around cheese ball, sealing cheese ball in meatball. Repeat with remaining chicken meatballs and cheese balls.

5 Preheat air fryer at 350°F for 3 minutes.

6 **To make Breading:** Combine bread crumbs and salt in a shallow dish. Roll stuffed meatballs in bread crumbs.

7 Add meatballs to air fryer basket lightly greased with preferred cooking oil and cook 5 minutes. Flip meatballs. Brush with melted butter. Cook an additional 5 minutes.

8 Transfer meatballs to a serving dish.

Pork Dust Chicken Livers

Although chicken livers are considered a delicacy not commonly enjoyed in a typical weekday meal, the price point of these little gems is surprisingly low. Soaking the livers in milk for an hour or two before cooking will help remove some of the bitter taste. And, if you have an orange in your kitchen, try giving the final air-fried livers a quick squeeze of citrus!

- **Hands-On Time:** 10 minutes
- **Cook Time:** 32 minutes

Serves 2

1 pound chicken livers, rinsed, connective tissue discarded
1 cup whole milk
½ cup cornmeal
¾ cup gluten-free all-purpose flour
1 teaspoon salt
1 teaspoon Cajun seasoning
2 large eggs
1½ cups pork dust
1 tablespoon olive oil

WHAT THE HECK IS PORK DUST?

Pork dust is simply pork rinds, or chicharrones, that have been ground down into a bread crumb consistency. Though the dust is sold in most stores, you can make it at home by simply pulsing a handful of pork rinds in a food processor to desired consistency. Use in place of bread crumbs or to lend another note of flavor to your dish.

1 Pat livers dry with paper towels, then transfer to a small bowl with milk. Refrigerate covered 2 hours.

2 In a shallow dish, combine cornmeal, flour, salt, and Cajun seasoning.

3 In a separate small bowl, whisk eggs.

4 In another shallow dish add pork dust.

5 Preheat air fryer at 375°F for 3 minutes.

6 Dredge one liver in cornmeal mixture. Dip in eggs. Dredge in pork dust. Repeat with remaining livers.

7 Add half of livers to air fryer basket lightly greased with preferred cooking oil. Brush tops of livers lightly with oil. Cook 8 minutes. Flip livers. Brush other side of livers with oil. Cook an additional 8 minutes.

8 Transfer cooked livers to a large serving dish and repeat with remaining livers. Serve warm.

Green Chile Chicken Quesadillas

Green chilies are mild and lend a beautiful acidity to any dish. Here, they complement the spiciness of the chili powder and the creaminess of the cheese. The chicken takes on all of these flavors and adds lean protein to these crispy quesadilla treats.

- **Hands-On Time: 10 minutes**
- **Cook Time: 12 minutes**

Serves 4

¾ cup sour cream

2 teaspoons chili powder

2 cups cooked boneless, skinless chicken breast, shredded

1 (7-ounce) can diced green chilies, including juice

½ teaspoon salt

3 tablespoons butter, melted

8 (6") gluten-free flour tortillas

2 cups grated Mexican cheese blend

1 Combine sour cream and chili powder in a small bowl. Refrigerate covered until ready to serve.

2 In a medium bowl, combine chicken, green chilies, and salt. Set aside.

3 Preheat air fryer to 350°F for 3 minutes.

4 Lightly brush melted butter on one side of a tortilla. Place tortilla butter side down in ungreased air fryer basket. Layer one-quarter of chicken mixture on tortilla, followed by one-quarter of cheese. Top with second tortilla. Lightly butter top of second tortilla.

5 Cook quesadilla 3 minutes.

6 Transfer cooked quesadilla to a large plate and repeat with remaining three quesadillas. Slice each quesadilla into six sections. Serve warm with sour cream mixture on the side for dipping.

Spaghetti Pie

Serve a slice of this Spaghetti Pie alongside a mixed salad for a twist on the typical spaghetti dinner. The gluten-free spaghetti forms the "crust" of this savory pie. The ricotta can also be subbed out for cottage cheese, and ground pork or beef can be used in place of the chicken. Let the ingredients of your kitchen help guide how you personalize your pie!

- **Hands-On Time:** 15 minutes
- **Cook Time:** 22 minutes

Serves 4

For Ricotta Cheese Layer
⅔ cup ricotta cheese
1 tablespoon grated Parmesan cheese
½ teaspoon salt

For Spaghetti Crust
2 tablespoons butter, melted
1 large egg
½ cup grated Parmesan cheese
¼ teaspoon salt
6 ounces dry gluten-free spaghetti, cooked according to instructions

For Toppings
2 teaspoons olive oil
⅓ cup diced peeled yellow onion
⅓ cup diced seeded green bell pepper
¼ pound ground chicken
1 cup marinara sauce
½ cup grated mozzarella cheese

1 **To make Ricotta Cheese Layer:** In a small bowl, combine Ricotta Cheese Layer ingredients.

2 **To make Spaghetti Crust:** In a large bowl, combine butter, egg, Parmesan, and salt. Add drained, cooled cooked spaghetti to bowl. Stir to combine. Set aside.

3 **To make Toppings:** In a medium skillet over medium heat, heat olive oil 30 seconds. Add onion and bell pepper and cook 3 minutes until onions are translucent. Add chicken and stir-fry until no longer pink, about 5 minutes.

4 **To put Spaghetti Pie together:** Preheat air fryer at 350°F for 3 minutes.

5 Gently press spaghetti mixture into a 7" springform pan lightly greased with preferred cooking oil. Spread ricotta mixture evenly on top. Top with toppings mixture, followed by marinara sauce.

6 Place springform pan in air fryer basket. Cook 10 minutes.

7 Spread mozzarella cheese evenly on top. Cook an additional 4 minutes.

8 Transfer pan to a cutting board and let rest 20 minutes. Once set, release sides of springform pan. Slice and serve pie.

Buttermilk-Brined Cornish Hen

When you don't want all of the meat a whole chicken provides, or you are entertaining and want a special entrée, the Cornish hen fits the bill.

- **Hands-On Time:** 10 minutes
- **Cook Time:** 28 minutes

Serves 2

2 cups buttermilk

1 teaspoon salt

1 teaspoon ground black pepper

½ teaspoon ground celery seed

1 Cornish hen (approximately 2 pounds)

1 tablespoon olive oil

½ medium lime, halved

2 cloves garlic, peeled and halved

2 sprigs fresh rosemary

1 In a medium bowl, combine buttermilk, salt, pepper, and celery seed. Add Cornish hen and toss in mixture. Refrigerate covered 2 hours up to overnight.

2 Preheat air fryer at 350°F for 3 minutes.

3 Pat hen dry with paper towels. Drizzle oil over top and inside hen. Stuff lime, garlic, and rosemary sprigs into hen cavity.

4 Place hen in ungreased air fryer basket. Cook 10 minutes. Flip hen. Cook 10 minutes. Flip hen once more and cook an additional 8 minutes. Use a meat thermometer to ensure internal temperature is at least 165°F. If below 165°F, continue cooking in 2-minute intervals until temperature is reached.

5 Transfer hen to a cutting board and let rest 5 minutes, then discard lime, garlic cloves, and rosemary. Cut down spine of hen and serve warm.

6

Beef and Pork Main Dishes

Full of flavor and naturally gluten-free, beef and pork crisp up nicely in the air fryer and are fantastic additions to a gluten-free lifestyle. Containing lots of protein and healthy fats (two of the three macronutrients your body needs to thrive), these are two foods you won't want to miss out on. The fan of the air fryer circulates the hot air around the meat, creating a crispy exterior while cooking the interior with a juicy result. And thanks to the air fryer, you have plenty of easy, tasty options.

With recipes ranging from Simple Filet Mignon and Fresh Steak Salad to Cereal-Crusted Pork Chops and Crispy Orange Pork over Rice, this chapter will help get you started with some classic air fryer beef and pork recipes, as well as introduce you to new favorites. Dig in!

Montreal Ribeye Steak

If garnishing a steak with dill sounds strange, read on. Montreal steak seasoning actually contains some dry dill. The fresh dill garnish pulls out those dried herb notes more, and lends a new flavor to the juicy ribeye steak.

- **Hands-On Time:** 5 minutes
- **Cook Time:** 10 minutes

Serves 2

1 tablespoon water

1 (12-ounce) ribeye steak, 1" thick

2 teaspoons Montreal steak seasoning

1 tablespoon unsalted butter, cut in half

1 teaspoon chopped fresh dill

1 Preheat air fryer at 400°F for 3 minutes.

2 Add water to bottom of air fryer.

3 Season steak on both sides with Montreal steak seasoning. Place steak in air fryer basket lightly greased with preferred cooking oil and cook 5 minutes. Flip steak and cook an additional 5 minutes until medium rare.

4 Transfer cooked steak to a cutting board and top with butter halves. Let rest 5 minutes, then garnish with fresh dill and serve.

WHAT IS MONTREAL STEAK SEASONING?

This is a classic, robust seasoning blend that can be purchased premixed in most grocery stores. To make your own, simply blend together 1 tablespoon ground black pepper, 1 tablespoon garlic powder, 1 tablespoon salt, 1 tablespoon smoked paprika, 1½ teaspoons ground mustard, 1½ teaspoons ground coriander, 1½ teaspoons dried dill, and 1½ teaspoons cayenne pepper.

Garlicky Strip Steak

When the months are cold and the grill is covered, the air fryer is a simple way to yield a perfect steak with a seared exterior and juicy interior.

- **Hands-On Time:** 5 minutes
- **Cook Time:** 8 minutes

Serves 2

3 cloves garlic, peeled and minced
1 tablespoon lemon juice
1 tablespoon olive oil
½ teaspoon salt
1 (¾-pound) strip steak

1 Combine garlic, lemon juice, olive oil, and salt in a small bowl. Brush mixture over steak, then cover and refrigerate steak 30 minutes.

2 Preheat air fryer at 400°F for 3 minutes.

3 Place steak in air fryer basket lightly greased with preferred cooking oil and cook 4 minutes. Flip steak and cook an additional 4 minutes until medium rare.

4 Transfer steak to a cutting board and let rest 5 minutes before serving.

Simple Filet Mignon

All you need for a perfect filet mignon is salt and pepper to let its natural flavor shine through. Don't forget to let the meat rest after cooking to avoid dry beef. The rest time allows the juices to settle back into the meat, while cutting a steak immediately drains those precious juices.

- **Hands-On Time:** 5 minutes
- **Cook Time:** 12 minutes

Serves 2

2 (8-ounce) filet mignon steaks, 1½″ thick
2 teaspoons salt
1 teaspoon ground black pepper
1 tablespoon unsalted butter, cut in half

1 Preheat air fryer at 375°F for 3 minutes.

2 Season steaks on both sides with salt and pepper.

3 Place steak in air fryer basket lightly greased with preferred cooking oil and cook 4 minutes. Flip steak and cook an additional 4 minutes. Flip steak one more time and cook 4 more minutes until medium rare.

4 Transfer steaks to a cutting board and top each with half of butter. Let rest 5 minutes before serving.

Mediterranean Short Ribs

Ribs can seem like a daunting meal to prepare, but short ribs fit perfectly into your air fryer. Let the Mediterranean marinade and air fryer do all the heavy lifting for you! This recipe yields juicy ribs with a crunchy sear on the outside. For an added flare, garnish with fresh basil leaves.

- **Hands-On Time:** 10 minutes
- **Cook Time:** 16 minutes

Serves 2

¼ cup olive oil

¼ cup balsamic vinegar

¼ cup chopped fresh basil leaves

¼ cup chopped fresh oregano

⅛ teaspoon Worcestershire sauce

3 cloves garlic, peeled and quartered

½ teaspoon salt

1 pound beef short ribs

1   In a large plastic resealable bag, combine olive oil, balsamic vinegar, basil, oregano, Worcestershire sauce, garlic, and salt. Set aside 2 tablespoons of mixture in a small bowl.

2   Add short ribs to bag and massage mixture into ribs. Seal bag and refrigerate 30 minutes up to overnight.

3   Preheat air fryer at 325°F for 3 minutes.

4   Place ribs in ungreased air fryer basket. Cook 8 minutes. Flip ribs and brush with extra sauce, then cook an additional 8 minutes.

5   Transfer ribs to a large serving plate.

Chimichurri Flank Steak

If you ever hear someone say they don't like flank steak, you can be sure that they are just cutting it wrong. It is imperative that you slice this cut of beef thin and against the grain. And although it is less expensive than the filet mignon or ribeye, you will feel like royalty. The Chimichurri Sauce lends layers of additional flavor.

- **Hands-On Time:** 5 minutes
- **Cook Time:** 19 minutes

Serves 4

For Marinade
⅔ cup olive oil
Juice of 1 medium orange
1 teaspoon orange zest
Juice of 1 lime
1 teaspoon lime zest
⅓ cup tamari sauce
2 tablespoons red wine vinegar
4 cloves garlic, peeled and minced
1 (1-pound) flank steak

For Chimichurri Sauce
1 cup fresh Italian parsley leaves
¼ cup fresh cilantro leaves
¼ cup fresh oregano leaves
¼ cup olive oil
½ small yellow onion, peeled and diced
4 cloves garlic, peeled and minced
2 tablespoons lime juice
2 teaspoons lime zest
2 tablespoons red wine vinegar
⅛ teaspoon cayenne pepper
½ teaspoon ground cumin
½ teaspoon salt

1 **To make Marinade:** Combine olive oil, orange juice, orange zest, lime juice, lime zest, tamari sauce, red wine vinegar, and garlic in a medium bowl or gallon-sized plastic resealable bag. Add flank steak and toss. Refrigerate 1 hour up to overnight.

2 **To make Chimichurri Sauce:** Place Chimichurri Sauce ingredients in a food processor or blender. Pulse several times until desired consistency. Refrigerate covered until ready to use.

3 Preheat air fryer at 325°F for 3 minutes.

4 Place steak in air fryer basket lightly greased with preferred cooking oil and cook 10 minutes. Flip steak and cook an additional 9 minutes until medium rare.

5 Transfer steak to a cutting board. Let rest 5 minutes, then slice thinly against the grain. Serve with Chimichurri Sauce.

Jamaican Jerk Meatballs

Mixing beef and pork adds an extra layer of flavor and fat to a dish. If you don't like spice, you can eliminate the habanero. You'll still feel like calling everyone "mahn."

- **Hands-On Time:** 10 minutes
- **Cook Time:** 16 minutes

Yields 18 meatballs

1 slice gluten-free sandwich bread, torn into bite-sized pieces

2 tablespoons whole milk

½ pound ground beef

½ pound ground pork

1 large egg

2 tablespoons finely diced peeled yellow onion

1 teaspoon minced seeded habanero

1 teaspoon Jamaican jerk seasoning

½ lime

1 Preheat air fryer at 350°F for 3 minutes.

2 Add bread to a large bowl with milk and toss. Add remaining ingredients except lime.

3 Use your hands to squeeze ingredients together until fully combined. Form mixture into eighteen meatballs, about 2 tablespoons each.

4 Add half of meatballs to air fryer basket lightly greased with preferred cooking oil and cook 6 minutes. Flip meatballs. Cook an additional 2 minutes.

5 Transfer cooked meatballs to a large serving dish. Repeat with remaining meatballs. Squeeze lime over meatballs and serve.

Fresh Steak Salad

You don't have to break the bank taking your family to an expensive steakhouse. Simply open your air fryer and a bottle of cabernet and break out some toasted gluten-free bread for an exceptionally delicious meal. And if you don't have pecans, throw in some walnuts instead. Pepitas can also replace the sunflower seeds, and if strawberries aren't in season, add in a fruit that is!

- **Hands-On Time:** 5 minutes
- **Cook Time:** 19 minutes

Serves 4

¼ cup olive oil

1 teaspoon + ⅛ teaspoon salt, divided

½ teaspoon + ⅛ teaspoon ground black pepper, divided

1 (1-pound) flank steak

¼ cup balsamic vinaigrette

1 tablespoon Dijon mustard

8 cups baby arugula

4 tablespoons crumbled blue cheese

½ medium red onion, peeled and cut into thin strips

4 tablespoons pecan pieces

4 tablespoons sunflower seeds

1 cup sliced hulled strawberries

1 Combine olive oil, 1 teaspoon salt, and ½ teaspoon pepper in a medium bowl or gallon-sized plastic resealable bag. Add flank steak and toss. Refrigerate 30 minutes up to overnight.

2 Preheat air fryer at 325°F for 3 minutes.

3 Place steak in air fryer basket lightly greased with preferred cooking oil and cook 10 minutes. Flip steak and cook an additional 9 minutes until medium rare.

4 Transfer steak to a cutting board. Let rest 5 minutes, then slice thinly across the grain.

5 While steak is resting, whisk balsamic vinaigrette with Dijon mustard in a large bowl. Add arugula and season with remaining salt and pepper. Toss, then divide into four serving bowls.

6 Top each salad with blue cheese, red onion, pecans, sunflower seeds, strawberries, and sliced steak. Serve immediately.

Beefy Bean Chili Pie

With meat, beans, and spices baked into a casserole and topped with gooey cheese, this meal has it all going on. Place a dollop of sour cream on this pie, garnish it with cilantro or parsley, and serve it with gluten-free corn muffins for an extraordinary experience.

- **Hands-On Time: 15 minutes**
- **Cook Time: 11 minutes**

Serves 4

2 teaspoons olive oil
½ pound ground beef
½ small yellow onion, peeled and diced
1 small carrot, peeled and diced
1 medium celery stalk, diced
1 (16-ounce) can chili beans in chili sauce
½ cup canned fire-roasted diced tomatoes, drained
½ teaspoon ground cumin
½ teaspoon chili powder
¼ teaspoon salt
1 cup corn chips
½ cup grated Mexican cheese blend

1 In a large skillet over medium-high heat, heat oil 30 seconds, then add beef, onion, carrot, and celery. Cook 5 minutes until beef is no longer pink. Drain fat from pan.

2 Stir in beans including sauce, diced tomatoes, cumin, chili powder, and salt. Remove from heat.

3 Preheat air fryer at 350°F for 3 minutes.

4 Spoon beef mixture into an ungreased 7" round cake barrel. Evenly distribute corn chips on top, followed by cheese. Place pan in air fryer basket and cook 6 minutes.

5 Remove pan from air fryer and let rest 10 minutes. Serve warm.

Steak Tacos with Pickled Radishes

Overflowing with flavor, you will think these steak tacos came straight off a gourmet food truck. Cutting the air-fried flank steak against the grain makes this more affordable cut of meat taste like it is the highest-priced beef from the butcher shop. The coolness of the cabbage and pico-guacamole is soothing against the zing of the pickled radishes. Top with hot sauce, guacamole, sour cream, or for even more flavor, Sriracha Mayonnaise (Chapter 3).

- **Hands-On Time:** 5 minutes
- **Cook Time:** 19 minutes

Yields 10 tacos

For Quick Pickled Radishes
5 medium radishes, julienned
2 tablespoons white wine vinegar
½ teaspoon granulated sugar
⅛ teaspoon salt

For Tacos
¼ cup olive oil
½ teaspoon salt
½ teaspoon ground cumin
1 (1-pound) flank steak
10 (4") mini gluten-free flour tortillas
1 cup shredded red cabbage

1 **To make Quick Pickled Radishes:** In a small bowl, combine Quick Pickled Radishes ingredients and refrigerate covered until ready to use.

2 **To make Tacos:** In a large bowl, combine olive oil, salt, and cumin. Add flank steak and toss. Refrigerate covered 30 minutes.

3 Preheat air fryer at 325°F for 3 minutes.

4 Place steak in ungreased air fryer basket and cook 10 minutes. Flip steak, then cook an additional 9 minutes until medium rare.

5 Transfer steak to a large cutting board and let rest 5 minutes. Slice thinly against the grain.

6 Build tacos by adding steak slices to flour tortillas along with red cabbage and pickled radishes. Serve immediately.

Southwest Steak Quesadillas

The air fryer cooks the ribeye perfectly, giving it a seared exterior and a juicy center. And the peppers and gooey cheese make these crowd-pleasing quesadillas simply delicious. Serve with some sour cream, diced tomatoes, or homemade guacamole for a full Southwest experience!

- **Hands-On Time:** 15 minutes
- **Cook Time:** 29 minutes

Serves 4

1 teaspoon chili powder

½ teaspoon smoked paprika

½ teaspoon ground cumin

¼ teaspoon garlic powder

½ teaspoon salt

¼ teaspoon ground black pepper

1 (12-ounce) ribeye steak, 1" thick

2 teaspoons olive oil

1 small red bell pepper, seeded and diced

1 small green bell pepper, seeded and diced

½ medium red onion, peeled and sliced

1 cup corn kernels

3 tablespoons butter, melted

8 (6") gluten-free flour tortillas

2 cups grated Monterey jack cheese

1 In a small bowl, combine chili powder, smoked paprika, cumin, garlic powder, salt, and black pepper. Rub ribeye on all sides with mixture. Refrigerate ribeye covered 30 minutes.

2 Preheat air fryer at 400°F for 3 minutes.

3 Place steak in air fryer basket lightly greased with preferred cooking oil and cook 5 minutes. Flip steak and cook an additional 5 minutes until medium rare.

4 Transfer steak to a cutting board and let rest 5 minutes.

5 While steak is resting, sauté olive oil with bell peppers and onion in a large skillet over medium-high heat 7 minutes until peppers are tender. Toss in corn. Set aside.

6 Thinly slice steak against the grain.

7 Preheat air fryer to 350°F for 3 minutes.

8 Lightly brush melted butter on one side of a tortilla. Place tortilla butter side down in ungreased air fryer basket. Layer one-quarter steak on tortilla, followed by one-quarter pepper mixture and one-quarter cheese. Top with second tortilla. Lightly butter top of quesadilla. Cook 3 minutes.

9 Transfer cooked quesadilla to a large plate and repeat with remaining three quesadillas. Slice each quesadilla into six sections. Serve warm.

Red Pepper Jelly and Cream Cheese Sliders

These sliders are inspired by a popular 1990s appetizer. Remember that block of cream cheese with the red pepper jelly on top? Well, now you can enjoy those flavors in these updated sliders!

- **Hands-On Time:** 5 minutes
- **Cook Time:** 18 minutes

Yields 8 sliders

½ pound ground beef
½ pound ground pork
½ teaspoon salt
8 tablespoons cream cheese
8 gluten-free slider buns
¼ cup red pepper jelly
½ cup fresh arugula

1 In a medium bowl, combine beef, pork, and salt. Form mixture into eight balls.

2 Roll 1 tablespoon cream cheese into a ball and press into center of one ball. Seal edges and gently press meat into a patty shape. Make a slight indention in middle of patty. Repeat with remaining cream cheese and balls.

3 Preheat air fryer at 350°F for 3 minutes.

4 Place four patties in air fryer basket lightly greased with preferred cooking oil. Cook 4 minutes. Flip patties and cook an additional 5 minutes.

5 Transfer cooked patties to four gluten-free buns. Repeat with remaining patties. Top patties with red pepper jelly and arugula leaves.

Honey Miso–Glazed Pork Loin Roast

The variety of flavors in this dish, from honey and sesame oil to ginger and garlic, may seem good enough. However, not so fast: the red miso also lends a brilliant touch of umami to the pork glaze.

- **Hands-On Time:** 10 minutes
- **Cook Time:** 40 minutes

Serves 6

3 tablespoons red miso paste

2 tablespoons honey

1 tablespoon sesame oil

¼ teaspoon ground ginger

2 cloves garlic, peeled and minced

½ teaspoon salt

½ teaspoon ground white pepper

1 (2-pound) boneless pork loin

1 Preheat air fryer at 350°F for 3 minutes.

2 In a small bowl, whisk together miso, honey, sesame oil, ground ginger, garlic, salt, and pepper. Massage mixture into all sides of pork loin.

3 Place pork in air fryer basket lightly greased with preferred cooking oil. Cook 20 minutes. Flip pork and cook an additional 20 minutes. Use a meat thermometer to ensure internal temperature is at least 145°F.

4 Transfer pork to a cutting board to rest 5 minutes before slicing and serving warm.

Cherry Barbecue Pork Chops

Fruit pairs so nicely with pork chops, and this recipe won't let you down. The air fryer sears all sides of the meat while keeping the inside juicy!

- **Hands-On Time:** 5 minutes
- **Cook Time:** 12 minutes

Serves 2

2 tablespoons cherry preserves

1 tablespoon ketchup

1 tablespoon Dijon mustard

2 teaspoons light brown sugar

1 teaspoon Worcestershire sauce

1 tablespoon lime juice

1 tablespoon olive oil

2 cloves garlic, peeled and minced

2 (10-ounce) bone-in pork chops, 1" thick

1 In a medium bowl, whisk together cherry preserves, ketchup, Dijon mustard, brown sugar, Worcestershire sauce, lime juice, olive oil, and garlic. Add pork chops to mixture and toss. Refrigerate covered 30 minutes.

2 Preheat air fryer at 350°F for 3 minutes.

3 Place pork chops in air fryer basket lightly greased with preferred cooking oil. Cook 4 minutes. Flip chops. Cook 4 minutes. Flip chops once more and cook an additional 4 minutes. Use a meat thermometer to ensure internal temperature is at least 145°F.

4 Transfer pork to a cutting board to rest 5 minutes before serving warm.

Crispy Orange Pork over Rice

By thinly slicing the pork prior to cooking, you allow the air fryer to give this succulent meat crispy edges, which adds another dimension of flavor and texture to this simple dish.

- **Hands-On Time:** 10 minutes
- **Cook Time:** 17 minutes

Serves 4

½ cup freshly squeezed orange juice

2 tablespoons orange marmalade

1 tablespoon avocado oil

1 tablespoon tamari

2 teaspoons sriracha

1 teaspoon yellow mustard

1 (1-pound) pork shoulder, trimmed and thinly sliced into 1" strips

2 tablespoons water

4 cups cooked white rice

¼ cup chopped fresh cilantro

1 In a medium bowl, whisk together orange juice, orange marmalade, oil, tamari, sriracha, and yellow mustard. Set aside half of marinade.

2 Add pork strips to bowl with half of marinade and toss. Refrigerate covered 30 minutes.

3 Preheat air fryer at 350°F for 3 minutes.

4 Add water to bottom of air fryer. Add pork to ungreased air fryer basket and cook 5 minutes. Toss, then cook 6 minutes. Toss once more and cook an additional 6 minutes.

5 Transfer pork to a medium bowl and toss with remaining marinade. Serve over cooked rice and garnish with fresh cilantro.

Cereal-Crusted Pork Chops

The Parmesan coating sets these air-fried pork chops apart from any others you've cooked in the past. They're done in 12 minutes, but allow these to rest while you plate the rest of your food. By the time the plate makes it to the table, they will be ready to eat!

- **Hands-On Time:** 5 minutes
- **Cook Time:** 12 minutes

Serves 2

1 large egg

1 tablespoon Dijon mustard

¼ cup grated Parmesan cheese

¼ cup crushed gluten-free bran cereal

¼ teaspoon ground black pepper

2 (8-ounce) bone-in pork chops, 1" thick

1 Preheat air fryer at 350°F for 3 minutes.

2 In a small dish, whisk egg and Dijon mustard. In a separate shallow dish, combine Parmesan cheese, bran cereal, and black pepper.

3 Dip pork chops in egg mixture. Dredge in cereal mixture.

4 Place pork in air fryer basket lightly greased with preferred cooking oil. Cook 4 minutes. Flip pork. Cook 4 minutes. Flip once more and cook an additional 4 minutes. Use a meat thermometer to ensure internal temperature is at least 145°F.

5 Transfer pork to a cutting board and let rest 5 minutes before serving warm.

Quinoa and Mushroom-Stuffed Pork Loins

These tender pork loins stuffed with juicy onions and mushrooms, with added saltiness and fat from the bacon and earthy flavor from the spinach, hit all the notes for a complete meal.

- **Hands-On Time:** 5 minutes
- **Cook Time:** 18 minutes

Serves 3

3 slices uncooked bacon, diced

½ medium yellow onion, peeled and diced

½ cup diced white mushrooms

1 cup baby spinach

½ teaspoon salt

½ teaspoon ground black pepper

½ cup cooked quinoa

3 (1-pound) boneless center-cut pork loins, 1" thick, pocket cut in each loin

1 In a medium skillet over medium-high heat, cook bacon 3 minutes until fat is rendered but not crispy.

2 Add onion and mushrooms to skillet. Stir-fry 3 minutes until onions are translucent. Add spinach, salt, and pepper and continue to cook another 1 minute until spinach is wilted.

3 Remove skillet from heat. Add quinoa and combine.

4 Preheat air fryer at 350°F for 3 minutes.

5 Stuff quinoa mixture into each pork loin and place pork in air fryer basket lightly greased with preferred cooking oil. Cook 11 minutes. Use a meat thermometer to ensure internal temperature is at least 145°F.

6 Transfer pork to a cutting board and let rest 5 minutes before serving warm.

Tex-Mex Andouille Sausage Rice Bake

By air frying the ingredients in this recipe, the flavors marry together, joined in their happy union by the melted cheese. If you like things extra spicy, add a shake or two of your favorite hot sauce.

- **Hands-On Time:** 10 minutes
- **Cook Time:** 20 minutes

Serves 4

1 tablespoon olive oil

¼ cup finely diced peeled yellow onion

1 medium green bell pepper, seeded and diced

3 cups cooked wild rice

1 cup canned corn, drained

¼ cup mayonnaise

2 tablespoons sour cream

¼ cup crumbled queso fresco cheese

1 teaspoon chili powder

1 teaspoon salt

1 teaspoon ground black pepper

7 ounces cooked andouille sausage, cut into 1" sections

1 In a medium skillet over medium-high heat, heat olive oil 30 seconds. Add onion and bell pepper and cook 4 minutes until onions are translucent. Remove skillet from heat.

2 In a large bowl, combine wild rice, corn, mayonnaise, sour cream, queso fresco, chili powder, salt, and black pepper. Stir in onion and bell pepper mixture. Add sausage.

3 Preheat air fryer at 350°F for 3 minutes.

4 Transfer sausage and rice mixture to a 7" cake barrel lightly greased with preferred cooking oil. Place pan in air fryer basket. Cook 15 minutes.

5 Remove pot from air fryer and let rest 10 minutes. Serve warm.

Moo Shu Pork Lettuce Wraps

Thought to have originated in northern China, moo shu is a mix of seasoned meat and vegetables, typically served with pancakes that you roll up like soft tacos. These Moo Shu Pork Lettuce Wraps are a nod to those flavors and ingredients. The lettuce serves as a great replacement for the gluten-filled pancakes.

- **Hands-On Time:** 15 minutes
- **Cook Time:** 25 minutes

Serves 4

3 tablespoons cornstarch, divided

1 tablespoon water

2 tablespoons rice vinegar

3 tablespoons gluten-free hoisin sauce

1 teaspoon oyster sauce

1 teaspoon + 1 tablespoon sesame oil, divided

¼ teaspoon ground ginger

1 large egg

2 tablespoons gluten-free all-purpose flour

1 (1-pound) boneless pork loin, cut into 1″ cubes

1 (14-ounce) bag coleslaw mix

3 medium green onions, sliced

½ cup sliced shiitake mushrooms

8 iceberg lettuce leaves

ALL HOISIN SAUCE IS NOT CREATED EQUAL
Read ingredient labels carefully when choosing a hoisin sauce. Some brands use soy sauce instead of tamari, so the product is not 100 percent gluten-free.

1. In a small bowl, whisk together 1 tablespoon cornstarch and water. Set aside.

2. In a small saucepan over medium heat, combine rice vinegar, hoisin sauce, oyster sauce, 1 teaspoon sesame oil, and ground ginger. Cook 3 minutes, stirring continuously. Add cornstarch slurry and cook another 1 minute. Set aside to allow mixture to thicken.

3. In a medium bowl, whisk together egg, flour, and remaining cornstarch. Set aside.

4. Preheat air fryer at 350°F for 3 minutes.

5. Dredge pork cubes in egg mixture. Shake off any excess.

6. Add half of pork to air fryer basket lightly greased with preferred cooking oil. Cook 4 minutes. Shake basket gently. Cook an additional 4 minutes. Use a meat thermometer to ensure internal temperature is at least 145°F. Set cooked pork aside and repeat with remaining pork.

7. While pork is cooking, add remaining sesame oil to a large skillet. Add coleslaw mix, green onions, and mushrooms. Cook 5 minutes over medium heat until coleslaw is wilted. Remove from heat.

8. Transfer cooked pork to skillet with cooked coleslaw mix. Add sauce and toss until coated. Serve warm wrapped in lettuce leaves.

Bahn Mi Pork Cabbage Salad

A typical bahn mi is a sandwich filled with Vietnamese seasoned meat and pickled vegetables, served on a baguette. This salad mimics those flavors, making it an addictive recipe that you'll want to make over and over again!

- **Hands-On Time:** 10 minutes
- **Cook Time:** 17 minutes

Serves 4

For Crema
4 tablespoons sour cream
4 tablespoons mayonnaise
1 tablespoon lime juice
½ teaspoon salt

For Pork Marinade
1 tablespoon sesame oil
1 tablespoon tamari
2 teaspoons sriracha
2 teaspoons honey
1 (1") knob fresh ginger, peeled and minced
1 (1-pound) pork shoulder, trimmed and thinly sliced into 1"-thick strips

For Salad
4 medium radishes, julienned
1 medium shallot, peeled and thinly sliced
3 tablespoons rice vinegar
⅛ teaspoon salt
2 tablespoons water
2 medium carrots, peeled and shaved into long ribbons
4 cups shredded napa cabbage
¼ cup chopped fresh basil leaves
¼ cup chopped fresh mint leaves

1 **To make Crema:** In a small bowl, whisk together Crema ingredients. Refrigerate covered until ready to use.

2 **To make Pork Marinade:** In a medium bowl, whisk together sesame oil, tamari, sriracha, honey, and minced ginger. Set aside half of marinade in a medium bowl.

3 Add pork strips to bowl with remaining marinade and toss. Refrigerate covered until ready to use.

4 **To make Salad:** In another medium bowl add radishes, shallot, rice vinegar, and salt. Refrigerate covered until ready to use.

5 Preheat air fryer at 350°F for 3 minutes.

6 Add water to bottom of air fryer. Add pork to ungreased air fryer basket. Cook 5 minutes. Toss, then cook 6 minutes. Toss once more and cook an additional 6 minutes.

7 Transfer pork to bowl with reserved marinade and toss.

8 Add carrots to ungreased air fryer basket and cook 2 minutes.

9 Distribute cabbage, basil, and mint to four serving bowls. Top with pork, carrots, and radish mixture. Drizzle Crema over top and serve.

Country-Style Pork Ribs

These ribs are so tender and tasty with the addition of a very tame spice mixture that can be found in most pantries. A little sweet and a little savory, this mixture is a perfect dry rub that can be used not only on these ribs, but also on chicken.

- **Hands-On Time:** 10 minutes
- **Cook Time:** 40 minutes

Serves 4

1 teaspoon smoked paprika
1 teaspoon garlic powder
1 teaspoon dark brown sugar
½ teaspoon ground mustard
1 teaspoon salt
½ teaspoon ground black pepper
2 tablespoons water
2 tablespoons olive oil
2 pounds country-style pork ribs

1 In a small bowl, combine smoked paprika, garlic powder, brown sugar, ground mustard, salt, and pepper.

2 Preheat air fryer at 350°F for 3 minutes. Add water to bottom of fryer.

3 Massage olive oil into pork ribs. Season ribs with spice mixture.

4 Add pork to air fryer basket lightly greased with preferred cooking oil. Cook 40 minutes, flipping every 10 minutes.

5 Transfer cooked pork to a serving platter and serve warm.

WHAT ARE COUNTRY-STYLE PORK RIBS?
Interestingly, country-style pork ribs aren't actually cut from the ribs: they come from the end of the pork shoulder, which is also referred to as the pork butt! Regardless, these "ribs" are a boneless, fatty cut that are so very tender and worth a try. You're sure to come back for more!

Aloha SPAM Tacos with Pineapple Salsa

Your guests will be screaming "Mahalo!" (thank you) when you cook up this homage to the beautiful islands of Hawaii. Hawaii consumes more SPAM than any other US state, and the homemade salsa is a tasty nod to the islands' symbol, the pineapple, or *hala kahiki*.

- **Hands-On Time:** 15 minutes
- **Cook Time:** 7 minutes

Serves 3

For Pineapple Salsa
1 cup diced pineapple
½ cup fresh lime juice
1 tablespoon lime zest
2 medium Roma tomatoes, seeded and diced
¼ cup finely diced peeled red onion
1 medium avocado, peeled, pitted, and diced
¼ cup chopped fresh cilantro
¼ cup chopped fresh mint
1 teaspoon salt

For Tacos
1 (12-ounce) can SPAM, sliced into ¼"-thick fries
1 cup coleslaw mix
1 batch Sriracha Mayonnaise (Chapter 3)
6 (6") gluten-free flour tortillas

1 **To make Pineapple Salsa:** Combine salsa ingredients in a medium bowl and refrigerate covered until ready to use.

2 **To make Tacos:** Preheat air fryer at 375°F for 3 minutes.

3 Place SPAM fries in air fryer basket lightly greased with preferred cooking oil. Cook 3 minutes. Flip fries. Cook an additional 4 minutes. Transfer to a large plate.

4 Build tacos by adding cooked SPAM, coleslaw mix, Pineapple Salsa, and a squeeze of Sriracha Mayonnaise to tortillas.

Fried SPAM Cuban Hangover Sandwiches

After a late night out with the gang, sometimes you just don't have time the next day to wait out a hangover. These sandwiches are the ultimate cure. Enjoy with a glass of tomato juice, or even a Bloody Mary for a little "hair of the dog," and tackle your day like a champ!

- **Hands-On Time:** 10 minutes
- **Cook Time:** 20 minutes

Serves 2

½ (12-ounce) can SPAM, cut into 4 slices

4 teaspoons yellow mustard

4 slices gluten-free sandwich bread

8 slices deli ham

8 dill pickle chips

2 slices Swiss cheese

4 tablespoons butter, melted

1 Preheat air fryer at 375°F for 3 minutes.

2 Place SPAM slices in air fryer basket lightly greased with preferred cooking oil. Cook 3 minutes. Flip slices. Cook an additional 3 minutes. Transfer to a medium plate.

3 Preheat air fryer at 350°F for 3 minutes.

4 Assemble sandwiches by spreading 1 teaspoon mustard to each bread slice. Layer bottom bread slice with portioned SPAM, ham, dill pickle chips, and Swiss cheese. Place top bread slices on toppings.

5 Brush outside top and bottom of each sandwich with melted butter. Place one sandwich in ungreased air fryer basket and cook 3 minutes. Flip sandwich and cook an additional 3 minutes. Repeat with remaining sandwich. Serve warm.

Bratwurst and Sauerkraut

The air fryer gives the sauerkraut a crunch around the edges. You can substitute the beer in this recipe for an equal amount of beef broth and ⅛ teaspoon Worcestershire sauce.

- **Hands-On Time:** 7 minutes
- **Cook Time:** 21 minutes

Yields 5 bratwurst links

1 pound uncooked pork bratwurst, approximately 5 links, pierced with a fork

1 (12-ounce) gluten-free bottle lager beer

2 cups water

½ medium yellow onion, peeled and sliced

2 cups drained sauerkraut

2 tablespoons German mustard

1 Add bratwurst to a medium saucepan with beer, water, and onion. Bring to a boil over high heat. Reduce heat to medium and simmer 15 minutes. Drain.

2 Preheat air fryer at 400°F for 3 minutes.

3 Place bratwurst and onions in air fryer basket lightly greased with preferred cooking oil. Cook 3 minutes. Flip bratwurst. Add sauerkraut and cook an additional 3 minutes. Use a meat thermometer to ensure internal temperature of bratwurst is at least 160°F.

4 Transfer bratwurst, onions, and sauerkraut to a large plate and serve warm with mustard on the side.

Gochujang Pork Meatballs

The combination of gochujang and orange marmalade lends sweet and spicy notes to the yummy fattiness of the pork meatballs. Serve over rice with steamed vegetables on the side.

- **Hands-On Time:** 15 minutes
- **Cook Time:** 16 minutes

Yields 16 meatballs

1 pound ground pork

1 large egg

1 tablespoon gochujang

1 teaspoon tamari

¼ teaspoon ground ginger

¼ cup plain gluten-free bread crumbs

1 scallion, whites minced, greens sliced, divided

4 tablespoons orange marmalade

1 Preheat air fryer at 350°F for 3 minutes.

2 Combine pork, egg, gochujang, tamari, ginger, bread crumbs, and minced scallion whites in a large bowl. Form into sixteen meatballs.

3 Add eight meatballs to air fryer basket lightly greased with preferred cooking oil and cook for 6 minutes. Flip meatballs. Cook an additional 2 minutes. Transfer to a large plate. Repeat with remaining meatballs.

4 Serve meatballs warm, garnished with sliced scallion greens and marmalade.

Fish and Seafood Main Dishes

Seafood is one of those meals that gets ordered a lot at restaurants but is overlooked at home. A great source of protein and other nutrients, as well as low in calories, it is something to embrace in your own kitchen. A lot of home chefs are timid when it comes to cooking fish and shellfish, but set aside your fears now: they are some of the quickest, easiest meals you will cook in your air fryer. The air fryer yields a crispy topping on a juicy fillet. Also, your fried oyster, shrimp, fish stick, and calamari favorites can be enjoyed without all of the fatty cooking oil used in traditional deep-frying.

From Barbecue Fried Oysters to Shrimp Po' Boys, and Fish Taco Rice Noodle Bowls, this chapter covers a variety of delicious fish and shellfish recipes that will have you eating seafood on a regular basis. Enjoy!

Barbecue Fried Oysters

Choose your own favorite gluten-free barbecue sauce when air frying these delicious bivalves! Whether you have a hankering for spicy sauce, something with an Asian flair, or sweet honey barbecue, you make the choice.

- **Hands-On Time:** 10 minutes
- **Cook Time:** 16 minutes

Serves 2

½ cup gluten-free all-purpose flour

½ cup bottled gluten-free barbecue sauce

1 cup gluten-free plain panko bread crumbs, finely crushed

½ pound shelled raw oysters, drained and patted dry

½ teaspoon salt, divided

1 Add flour to a small bowl. Add barbecue sauce to another small bowl. Add bread crumbs to a separate shallow dish.

2 Preheat air fryer at 400°F for 3 minutes.

3 Roll oysters in flour. Shake off excess flour, then dredge oysters in barbecue sauce. Shake off excess sauce. Roll oysters in bread crumbs. Set aside on a large plate. Repeat with remaining oysters.

4 Add half of oysters to air fryer basket lightly greased with preferred cooking oil. Cook 4 minutes. Carefully flip oysters. Cook an additional 4 minutes.

5 Transfer cooked oysters to a large serving plate. Sprinkle with salt. Cook remaining oysters, then transfer to plate and sprinkle with remaining salt. Serve warm.

Fish Sticks

A kid favorite for years, fish sticks are typically coated in gluten-laden bread crumbs and other fillers. By making your own, you can ensure the ingredients are gluten-free and the fish is fresh. In addition, the air fryer eliminates the need for deep-frying. Serve with your favorite dipping sauce!

- **Hands-On Time: 10 minutes**
- **Cook Time: 20 minutes**

Serves 4

½ cup + ¼ cup gluten-free all-purpose flour, divided
1 large egg
¼ cup cornmeal
½ teaspoon salt
¼ teaspoon smoked paprika
1 pound boneless, skinless cod, cut into 1"-thick sticks

1. Add ½ cup flour to a small bowl. Whisk egg in another small bowl. Combine remaining flour, cornmeal, salt, and smoked paprika in a separate shallow dish.

2. Preheat air fryer at 350°F for 3 minutes.

3. Roll one fish stick in flour. Shake off excess flour, then dip fish stick in egg. Shake off excess egg. Roll fish stick in bread crumb mixture. Transfer to a large plate and repeat with remaining fish sticks.

4. Add half of fish sticks to air fryer basket lightly greased with preferred cooking oil. Cook 5 minutes. Carefully flip fish sticks. Cook an additional 5 minutes.

5. Transfer cooked fish sticks to a large serving plate and repeat with remaining fish sticks. Serve warm.

Fried Shrimp with Cocktail Sauce

Shrimp are naturally low in fat and calories. However, in the gluten-free lifestyle, you can sometimes miss the crunch that the deep-fried variety gives you, so you are tempted to eliminate shrimp from your diet entirely. Wait a minute! Delicious, crunchy, and yet somehow *not* deep-fried, these air-fried shrimp are a perfect replacement for those looking to eliminate gluten from their diet or reduce their fat intake.

- **Hands-On Time:** 10 minutes
- **Cook Time:** 8 minutes

Serves 2

For Cocktail Sauce

1 cup ketchup

2 tablespoons prepared horseradish

1 tablespoon lemon juice

½ teaspoon Worcestershire sauce

⅛ teaspoon Tabasco sauce

⅛ teaspoon chili powder

¼ teaspoon salt

⅛ teaspoon ground black pepper

For Shrimp

⅓ cup gluten-free all-purpose flour

2 tablespoons cornstarch

1 teaspoon salt

¼ cup whole milk

1 large egg

½ cup gluten-free plain panko bread crumbs

1 tablespoon Cajun seasoning

½ pound medium raw shrimp, tail on, deveined and shelled

1 **To make Cocktail Sauce:** Combine Cocktail Sauce ingredients in a small bowl. Refrigerate covered until ready to use.

2 **To make Shrimp:** In a medium bowl, combine flour, cornstarch, and salt. In another medium bowl, combine milk and egg. In a separate shallow dish, combine bread crumbs and Cajun seasoning.

3 Preheat air fryer at 375°F for 3 minutes.

4 Toss shrimp in flour mixture. Shake off excess flour. Dredge in egg mixture, then shake off excess. Dip in bread crumb mixture. Shake off excess.

5 Place shrimp in air fryer basket lightly greased with preferred cooking oil. Cook 4 minutes. Gently flip shrimp. Cook an additional 4 minutes.

6 Transfer cooked shrimp to a large plate and serve warm with Cocktail Sauce.

Prosciutto-Wrapped Shrimp Jalapeño Poppers

Because shrimp cook quickly, wrapping them in prosciutto instead of bacon still lends a salty, fatty flavor, but doesn't involve the extra cooking time needed for bacon. Stuffed with two kinds of cheeses and given a little kick from the jalapeños and other spices, these shrimp will be a favorite!

- **Hands-On Time:** 10 minutes
- **Cook Time:** 18 minutes

Yields 20 stuffed shrimp

- 3 tablespoons cream cheese, room temperature
- 2 tablespoons finely grated Cheddar cheese
- 2 medium jalapeños, seeded and small-diced
- ¼ teaspoon garlic powder
- 1 tablespoon mayonnaise
- ¼ teaspoon ground black pepper
- 2 tablespoons water
- 20 large raw shrimp (about 1 pound), deveined, shelled, tail on, and sliced down the spine
- 10 ounces prosciutto, cut into 20 slices
- ¼ cup chopped fresh parsley

1 In a medium bowl, combine cream cheese, Cheddar cheese, jalapeños, garlic powder, mayonnaise, and black pepper.

2 Preheat air fryer at 400°F for 3 minutes.

3 Evenly press cream cheese mixture into shrimp. Wrap 1 piece prosciutto around each shrimp to hold in cream cheese mixture.

4 Place half of wrapped shrimp in ungreased air fryer basket. Cook 5 minutes. Flip shrimp. Cook an additional 4 minutes.

5 Transfer cooked shrimp to a large serving plate. Repeat with remaining shrimp. Garnish with chopped parsley and serve warm.

Shrimp Po' Boys

Ooooh weeee: take a virtual trip to New Orleans without ever leaving your home, courtesy of these Shrimp Po' Boys. Don't skip the creamy Remoulade Sauce, as it pulls each sandwich together. And, if spice is your thing, add a few extra drops of Tabasco sauce.

- **Hands-On Time:** 10 minutes
- **Cook Time:** 18 minutes

Serves 2

For Remoulade Sauce
½ cup mayonnaise
1 tablespoon Dijon mustard
1 teaspoon smoked paprika
1 teaspoon Cajun seasoning
1 teaspoon prepared horseradish
½ teaspoon dill pickle juice
½ teaspoon Tabasco sauce
2 cloves garlic, peeled and minced

For Shrimp
⅓ cup gluten-free all-purpose flour
2 tablespoons cornstarch
1 teaspoon salt
¼ cup whole milk
1 large egg
½ cup gluten-free plain panko bread crumbs
1 tablespoon Old Bay seasoning
½ pound medium raw shrimp, tail on, deveined, and shelled

For Sandwiches
2 gluten-free hoagie rolls, split
3 tablespoons butter, melted
½ cup shredded iceberg lettuce
1 medium vine-ripe tomato, seeded and diced

1 **To make Remoulade Sauce:** In a small bowl, combine Remoulade Sauce ingredients. Refrigerate covered until ready to use.

2 **To make Shrimp:** In a medium bowl, combine flour, cornstarch, and salt. In another medium bowl, combine milk and egg. In a separate shallow dish, combine bread crumbs and Old Bay seasoning.

3 Preheat air fryer at 375°F for 3 minutes.

4 Toss shrimp in flour mixture. Shake off excess. Dredge in egg mixture, shake off excess, then dip in bread crumb mixture. Shake off excess.

5 Place half of shrimp in air fryer basket lightly greased with preferred cooking oil. Cook 4 minutes. Gently flip shrimp. Cook an additional 4 minutes.

6 Transfer cooked shrimp to a large serving plate. Repeat with remaining shrimp.

7 **To make Sandwiches:** Brush hoagie rolls with butter. Place both sides of one roll in ungreased air fryer basket and cook, butter side down, 1 minute. Repeat with remaining roll.

8 Make sandwiches by topping each with portioned shrimp, lettuce, tomatoes, and Remoulade Sauce.

Fish Sandwiches

Who needs fast-food, gluten-filled, deep-fried fish sandwiches when you can make your own that are fresh and gluten-free? The creamy homemade Tartar Sauce is essential to these simple sandwiches.

- **Hands-On Time:** 10 minutes
- **Cook Time:** 12 minutes

Serves 4

For Tartar Sauce
½ cup mayonnaise
1 tablespoon Dijon mustard
½ cup small-diced dill pickles
⅛ teaspoon salt
¼ teaspoon ground black pepper

For Fish
⅓ cup gluten-free all-purpose flour
2 tablespoons cornstarch
1 teaspoon smoked paprika
1 teaspoon salt
¼ cup whole milk
1 large egg
½ cup gluten-free plain panko bread crumbs
4 (6-ounce) cod fillets, cut in half

For Sandwiches
½ cup shredded iceberg lettuce
1 large vine-ripe tomato, seeded and sliced
4 gluten-free hamburger buns

1 **To make Tartar Sauce:** In a small bowl, combine Tartar Sauce ingredients. Refrigerate covered until ready to use.

2 **To make Fish:** Preheat air fryer at 375°F for 3 minutes.

3 In a medium bowl, combine flour, cornstarch, smoked paprika, and salt. Set side.

4 In a separate medium bowl, combine milk and egg. Set aside.

5 In a small shallow dish, add bread crumbs.

6 Toss cod pieces in flour mixture. Dredge in egg mixture, then dip in bread crumbs. Shake off excess after each step.

7 Place half of cod in air fryer basket lightly greased with preferred cooking oil. Cook 3 minutes. Gently flip fish, then cook an additional 3 minutes.

8 Transfer fish to a large serving plate. Repeat with remaining fish.

9 **To make Sandwiches:** Construct sandwiches by adding fish, lettuce, tomatoes, and Tartar Sauce to each bottom bun, then add top bun.

Seasoned Shrimp

These little guys are awesome on their own, but even better served over a bowl of grits!

- **Hands-On Time:** 5 minutes
- **Cook Time:** 6 minutes

Serves 2

1 pound medium raw shrimp, tail on, deveined, shelled, thawed

2 tablespoons butter, melted

2 teaspoons Cajun seasoning

1 tablespoon lemon juice (about ½ large lemon)

1 tablespoon grated Parmesan cheese

1 Preheat air fryer at 350°F for 3 minutes.

2 In a medium bowl, toss shrimp in melted butter. Season with Cajun seasoning.

3 Place seasoned shrimp in air fryer basket lightly greased with preferred cooking oil. Cook 4 minutes. Gently flip shrimp. Cook an additional 2 minutes.

4 Transfer cooked shrimp to a large plate. Squeeze lemon juice over shrimp. Toss with Parmesan cheese. Serve warm.

Fried Mustard Sardines

Sardines are quite delicious and packed with nutrition, including omega-3s, vitamin D, protein, and selenium. Plus, breading them and cooking them in the air fryer takes away the sometimes unappealing visual. As a bonus, they are affordable and low in mercury and other metals.

- **Hands-On Time:** 5 minutes
- **Cook Time:** 6 minutes

Serves 2

½ cup gluten-free plain panko bread crumbs

2 (3.75-ounce) cans boneless, skinless sardines in mustard sauce

2 lemon wedges

1 Preheat air fryer at 350°F for 3 minutes.

2 Place bread crumbs in a shallow dish. Roll sardines in dish to coat.

3 Place breaded sardines in air fryer basket lightly greased with preferred cooking oil. Cook 3 minutes. Gently flip sardines. Cook an additional 3 minutes.

4 Transfer sardines to a large serving dish and serve warm with lemon wedges.

Classic Tuna Melts

These classic sandwiches never go out of style! Serve with a light arugula salad or fresh slices of beefsteak tomato.

- **Hands-On Time:** 10 minutes
- **Cook Time:** 4 minutes

Serves 2

1 (6-ounce) can tuna in water, drained

¼ cup mayonnaise

2 teaspoons yellow mustard

2 tablespoons minced celery

1 tablespoon minced peeled yellow onion

⅛ teaspoon salt

⅛ teaspoon ground black pepper

2 gluten-free English muffins, split

4 slices American cheese

1 In a medium bowl, combine tuna, mayonnaise, mustard, celery, onion, salt, and pepper.

2 Preheat air fryer at 350°F for 3 minutes.

3 Distribute tuna salad among English muffin halves and spread. Top each half with one cheese slice.

4 Place muffin halves in ungreased air fryer basket and cook 4 minutes until cheese starts to brown. Remove and serve warm.

Crab Cakes

The problem with many store-bought crab cakes is that the breading overpowers the flavor of the beautiful crabmeat. Making your own subtler version is easy, thanks to the air fryer. With gently crisp edges and a succulent interior, this gourmet entrée is ready in minutes.

- **Hands-On Time:** 8 minutes
- **Cook Time:** 20 minutes

Yields 8 crab cakes

1 pound lump crabmeat, shells discarded

⅓ cup mayonnaise

1 teaspoon Dijon mustard

1 teaspoon lemon juice

1 tablespoon minced peeled yellow onion

½ cup plain gluten-free bread crumbs

2 tablespoons chopped fresh parsley

1 large egg

1 teaspoon Old Bay seasoning

⅛ teaspoon salt

1 Preheat air fryer at 400°F for 3 minutes.

2 In a medium bowl, combine crabmeat, mayonnaise, Dijon mustard, lemon juice, onion, bread crumbs, parsley, egg, Old Bay seasoning, and salt. Form mixture into eight patties.

3 Place half of patties in air fryer basket lightly greased with preferred cooking oil. Cook 5 minutes. Flip crab cakes. Cook an additional 5 minutes. Repeat with remaining patties.

4 Transfer cakes to a large serving dish and let rest 5 minutes before serving.

Crab Cakes Benedict

You don't need bread to make an eggs Benedict, and it doesn't have to be breakfast to enjoy poached eggs. Turn up the class and serve your eggs and silken hollandaise sauce atop luxurious crab cakes.

- **Hands-On Time:** 15 minutes
- **Cook Time:** 20 minutes

Serves 4

½ pound lump crabmeat, shells discarded

2 tablespoons mayonnaise

½ teaspoon yellow mustard

½ teaspoon lemon juice

½ tablespoon minced shallot

¼ cup plain gluten-free bread crumbs

1 large egg

⅛ teaspoon salt

⅛ teaspoon ground black pepper

4 poached eggs

½ cup hollandaise sauce

2 teaspoons chopped fresh chives

1 Preheat air fryer at 400°F for 3 minutes.

2 In a medium bowl, combine crabmeat, mayonnaise, mustard, lemon juice, shallots, bread crumbs, egg, salt, and pepper. Form mixture into four patties.

3 Place half of patties in air fryer basket lightly greased with preferred cooking oil. Cook 5 minutes. Flip patties. Cook an additional 5 minutes. Transfer crab cakes to a large serving dish. Repeat with remaining patties.

4 Gently place one poached egg atop each crab cake. Drizzle with hollandaise sauce and garnish with chives.

MAKE A QUICK BLENDER HOLLANDAISE SAUCE

Blend together 2 egg yolks, 2 teaspoons fresh lemon juice, ⅛ teaspoon salt, and ⅛ teaspoon cayenne pepper. With the blender running on low, slowly drizzle 6 tablespoons melted butter into mixture until frothy and thick.

Just for the Halibut with Lemon Aioli Coleslaw

This recipe features a simple fish with a tasty coleslaw, but it can also be turned into a quick fix for Taco Tuesday. Simply buy some gluten-free flour tortillas, dice up the cooked halibut, and top with the ultracreamy Lemon Aioli Coleslaw! Serve with lime wedges for squeezing.

- **Hands-On Time:** 10 minutes
- **Cook Time:** 20 minutes

Serves 4

For Lemon Aioli Coleslaw
1 (12-ounce) bag coleslaw mix
¼ cup mayonnaise
1 teaspoon horseradish mustard
1 teaspoon lemon zest
1 tablespoon lemon juice
¼ teaspoon salt

For Fish
4 (6-ounce) halibut fillets
1 teaspoon salt
½ teaspoon ground black pepper

1 **To make Lemon Aioli Coleslaw:** In a small bowl, combine coleslaw ingredients. Refrigerate covered until ready to use.

2 **To make Fish:** Preheat air fryer at 350°F for 3 minutes.

3 Season halibut fillets with salt and pepper. Place two fillets in air fryer basket lightly greased with preferred cooking oil. Cook 10 minutes until fish is opaque and flakes easily with a fork. Set aside.

4 Repeat with remaining fillets.

5 Transfer cooked halibut to serving plates and serve warm with chilled coleslaw.

Salmon Cakes with Dill Sauce

This recipe calls for canned salmon to make things easier; however, leftover cooked salmon or freshly cooked salmon flaked into pieces are perfect substitutes when preparing these omega-3 powerhouse patties. The Dill Sauce is divine, making this recipe a tasty and healthy lunch or dinner.

- **Hands-On Time:** 20 minutes
- **Cook Time:** 20 minutes

Serves 4

For Dill Sauce

¼ cup sour cream

2 tablespoons mayonnaise

2 cloves garlic, peeled and minced

2 tablespoons chopped fresh dill

2 teaspoons lime juice

¼ teaspoon salt

For Salmon Patties

1 (14.75-ounce) can salmon

½ cup mayonnaise

1 large egg

2 tablespoons finely minced seeded red bell pepper

½ cup gluten-free plain panko bread crumbs

⅛ teaspoon salt

1 Preheat air fryer at 400°F for 3 minutes.

2 **To make Dill Sauce:** In a small bowl, combine Dill Sauce ingredients. Refrigerate covered until ready to use.

3 **To make Salmon Patties:** In a medium bowl, combine Salmon Patties ingredients. Form mixture into eight patties.

4 Place half of patties in air fryer basket lightly greased with preferred cooking oil. Cook 5 minutes. Flip patties. Cook an additional 5 minutes. Transfer patties to a large serving dish and repeat with remaining patties.

5 Let rest 5 minutes before serving warm with Dill Sauce on the side.

Crab Dip–Stuffed Portabellas

Brimming with creamy, decadent crab dip, these portabella mushrooms are sure to be the star of any meal. Serve them with mixed greens lightly tossed with olive oil, a squeeze or two of lemon juice, and a little salt and pepper for a crab-tastic meal!

- **Hands-On Time:** 15 minutes
- **Cook Time:** 13 minutes

Serves 2

2 tablespoons butter, divided

¼ cup diced peeled red onion

6 ounces cream cheese, room temperature

1 tablespoon grated Parmesan cheese

½ teaspoon prepared horseradish

¼ teaspoon hot sauce

¼ teaspoon Worcestershire sauce

¼ teaspoon smoked paprika

⅛ teaspoon salt

6 ounces lump crabmeat, shells discarded

2 large portabella mushrooms, stems removed and black gills scraped

¼ cup plain gluten-free bread crumbs

1 In a medium skillet over medium heat, melt 1 tablespoon butter 30 seconds. Add red onion and cook 3 minutes until tender. Add cream cheese, Parmesan cheese, horseradish, hot sauce, Worcestershire sauce, smoked paprika, and salt. Cook 2 minutes until smooth.

2 Fold crabmeat into skillet mixture. Spoon mixture into mushroom caps. Set aside.

3 Preheat air fryer at 350°F for 3 minutes.

4 In a small bowl, melt remaining tablespoon butter. Stir in bread crumbs. Sprinkle bread crumb mixture over stuffed mushrooms.

5 Place stuffed mushrooms in air fryer basket lightly greased with preferred cooking oil and cook 8 minutes.

6 Transfer cooked mushrooms to a large plate and serve warm.

WHY SCRAPE THE GILLS FROM PORTABELLA CAPS?
Although edible, the black gills in portabella caps tend to hide dirt, lending a gritty texture to your meal. Also, they can turn your sauce or filling a murky brown color, which may give the dish an unappetizing appearance.

Sea Scallops with Creamy Caper Sauce

The air fryer perfectly sears these beautiful scallops on all sides. Serve with steamed asparagus, mashed potatoes, and a drizzle of fresh hollandaise sauce over everything for a decadent display of yummy!

- **Hands-On Time:** 5 minutes
- **Cook Time:** 15 minutes

Serves 2

For Creamy Caper Sauce
1 tablespoon olive oil

1 medium shallot, peeled and minced

2 tablespoons capers

2 cloves garlic, peeled and minced

½ cup heavy cream

1 tablespoon butter

1 tablespoon lemon juice

¼ teaspoon salt

½ teaspoon ground black pepper

For Scallops
2 tablespoons butter, melted and divided

1 pound jumbo sea scallops (about 10)

2 tablespoons chopped fresh parsley

1. **To make Creamy Caper Sauce:** In a small saucepan over medium heat, heat olive oil 30 seconds. Add shallots and stir-fry 2 minutes until translucent. Stir in remaining Creamy Caper Sauce ingredients, cooking 2 minutes to a rolling boil.

2. Reduce heat to a simmer on low and cook sauce 3 more minutes until it starts to thicken. Remove pan from heat.

3. **To make Scallops:** Preheat air fryer at 400°F for 3 minutes.

4. Place half of butter in a medium bowl and toss in scallops to coat all sides.

5. Place scallops in air fryer basket lightly greased with preferred cooking oil. Cook 2 minutes. Flip scallops. Cook 2 minutes.

6. Brush tops of scallops with remaining butter. Cook 2 more minutes. Flip scallops. Cook an additional 2 minutes.

7. Transfer cooked scallops to a large plate. Drizzle Creamy Caper Sauce over scallops, garnish with parsley, and serve warm.

Lobster Tails

If those big lobster tanks at the grocery store give you the heebie-jeebies and prevent you from cooking lobster at home, you're not alone. Luckily, most grocers also sell pre-cut 5- to 6-ounce lobster tails that make handling this shellfish much easier.

- **Hands-On Time:** 10 minutes
- **Cook Time:** 8 minutes

Serves 2

2 small uncooked lobster
   tails (about 6 ounces
   each), thawed
1 tablespoon butter, melted
½ teaspoon Old Bay
   Seasoning
1 tablespoon chopped fresh
   parsley
2 lemon wedges

1 Preheat air fryer at 400°F for 3 minutes.

2 Using kitchen shears, cut down middle of each lobster tail on softer side. Carefully run your finger between lobster meat and shell to loosen meat.

3 Place lobster tails in ungreased air fryer basket, cut side up. Cook 4 minutes. Brush tail meat with butter and sprinkle with Old Bay Seasoning. Cook an additional 4 minutes.

4 Transfer tails to a large plate and serve warm, garnished with parsley and lemon wedges.

MAKING BROTH WITH LOBSTER TAIL SHELLS

You can use those tail shells to make a tasty broth for lobster bisque, crab soup, or even a seafood gumbo. Place shells in a heavy-bottomed pot with 4 cups water, 1 peeled and diced medium yellow onion, 1 diced medium carrot, 1 diced medium celery stalk, and 2 peeled and halved garlic cloves. Bring to a boil over high heat, then reduce heat to a simmer and cover 30 minutes. Strain liquid into a large container and refrigerate up to four days or freeze up to six months.

Roasted Red Pepper Tilapia Roulade

Topping the roulade with crushed cornflakes adds a layer of texture that makes the simple ingredients in this elegant dish shine.

- **Hands-On Time:** 15 minutes
- **Cook Time:** 6 minutes

Serves 4

1 large egg
2 tablespoons water
1 cup crushed cornflakes
1 teaspoon salt
½ teaspoon ground black pepper
4 slices jarred roasted red pepper
4 (5-ounce) tilapia fillets, pounded to ¼" thickness
2 tablespoons butter, melted
4 lime wedges

1 Preheat air fryer at 350°F for 3 minutes.

2 In a small bowl, whisk together egg and water. In a separate shallow dish, combine cornflakes, salt, and black pepper.

3 Place one slice roasted red pepper on each fish fillet. Tightly and gently roll one fillet from one short end to the other. Secure with a toothpick. Repeat with remaining fillets.

4 Roll each fillet in egg mixture, then dredge in cornflake mixture.

5 Place fish in air fryer basket lightly greased with preferred cooking oil. Drizzle tops with melted butter. Cook 6 minutes.

6 Transfer fish to a large serving dish and let rest 5 minutes. Remove toothpicks. Serve warm with lime wedges on the side.

Lobster and Corn Salad Lettuce Wraps

The air fryer will work double duty in this recipe, cooking the lobster tails and corn at the same time. Mixed with freshly cut vegetables, tossed in a light dressing, and spooned into lettuce leaves, the lightness of this meal is best enjoyed alfresco!

- **Hands-On Time:** 15 minutes
- **Cook Time:** 8 minutes

Serves 2

2 small uncooked lobster tails (6 ounces each), thawed

1 large corn on the cob, husked and halved

1 tablespoon butter, melted

2 medium Roma tomatoes, seeded and diced

2 tablespoons diced peeled red onion

½ medium avocado, peeled, pitted, and diced

Juice of ½ lime

2 tablespoons plain Greek yogurt

2 tablespoons olive oil

½ teaspoon salt

¼ teaspoon ground black pepper

4 Bibb lettuce leaves

1 Preheat air fryer at 400°F for 3 minutes.

2 Using kitchen shears, cut down middle of each lobster tail on softer side. Carefully run your finger between lobster meat and shell to loosen meat.

3 Place corn halves in air fryer basket lightly greased with preferred cooking oil. Place tails on top of corn, cut side up. Cook 4 minutes. Brush lobster meat with butter. Cook an additional 4 minutes.

4 Transfer corn and lobster to a large plate. When cool enough to handle, about 5 minutes, cut corn from cob and remove lobster meat from shells. Dice lobster meat.

5 In a medium bowl, combine corn kernels, diced lobster, tomatoes, red onion, avocado, lime juice, yogurt, olive oil, salt, and pepper. Distribute mixture among lettuce leaves and serve.

Cape Cod Crusted Cod

Certified gluten-free, Cape Cod Potato Chips are already seasoned and make a tasty accompaniment to any meal. When crumbled, these chips are the perfect crust for the nonfishy, flaky cod filets.

- **Hands-On Time:** 10 minutes
- **Cook Time:** 10 minutes

Serves 2

½ cup crushed Cape Cod Potato Chips, Original

1 teaspoon chopped fresh tarragon

⅛ teaspoon salt

1 tablespoon Dijon mustard

1 teaspoon lemon juice

1 tablespoon butter, melted

2 (6-ounce) boneless, skinless cod fillets

1 Preheat air fryer at 350°F for 3 minutes.

2 In a small bowl, combine potato chips, tarragon, salt, mustard, lemon juice, and butter. Press potato chip mixture evenly across tops of cod.

3 Place fish in air fryer basket lightly greased with preferred cooking oil. Cook 10 minutes until fish is opaque and flakes easily with a fork.

4 Transfer cooked fish to serving plates and serve warm.

Berbere Sea Bass

The savory blend of spices in berbere pairs nicely with the simple, buttery sea bass. You can find this Ethiopian blend in some grocery stores or online. It is also wonderful on chicken and pork!

- **Hands-On Time:** 5 minutes
- **Cook Time:** 7 minutes

Serves 2

1 teaspoon olive oil
2 (6-ounce) boneless,
    skinless sea bass fillets,
    about 1" thick
½ teaspoon berbere
    seasoning
2 teaspoons chopped fresh
    cilantro
4 lemon quarters

1 Preheat air fryer at 375°F for 3 minutes.

2 Rub oil over fillets. Sprinkle fillets with berbere seasoning.

3 Place fillets in air fryer basket lightly greased with preferred cooking oil. Cook 7 minutes.

4 Transfer cooked fillets to serving plates and let rest 5 minutes. Garnish with cilantro and place lemon quarters on the side to squeeze over fillets. Serve warm.

Super Simple Salmon

It is well known that salmon is a great source of omega-3 fatty acids, but sometimes it can be daunting to prepare at home. The air fryer makes things easy by not only cooking a juicy piece of fish, but also crisping up the skin to perfection!

- **Hands-On Time:** 5 minutes
- **Cook Time:** 7 minutes

Serves 4

2 (6-ounce) boneless,
    skinless salmon fillets,
    about 1" thick, patted dry
½ teaspoon salt
1 tablespoon butter, cut in
    half
4 lemon slices

1 Preheat air fryer at 375°F for 3 minutes.

2 Season fillets with salt. Top each with half of butter and lemon slices.

3 Place salmon, skin side down, in air fryer basket lightly greased with preferred cooking oil. Cook 7 minutes.

4 Transfer fillets to serving plates and serve warm.

Miso-Glazed Salmon Fillets with Brown Rice

Enhanced by the tamari, garlic powder, and brown sugar, the miso paste in this recipe offers an earthy and salty note to the beautiful glaze. Salmon has never tasted so savory and filled with umami flavor! Steam some broccoli as a side to round out this meal.

- **Hands-On Time:** 5 minutes
- **Cook Time:** 7 minutes

Serves 4

1 tablespoon sesame oil
2 tablespoons miso paste
2 tablespoons tamari
2 tablespoons dark brown sugar
½ teaspoon garlic powder
4 (6-ounce) boneless, skinless salmon fillets, about 1" thick
4 cups cooked brown rice

1 Whisk together sesame oil, miso paste, tamari, brown sugar, and garlic powder in a small bowl. Place one-third of marinade in a shallow dish and dunk salmon fillets in mixture to coat. Refrigerate covered 10 minutes. Set aside remaining marinade.

2 Preheat air fryer at 375°F for 3 minutes.

3 Place salmon, skin side up, in air fryer basket lightly greased with preferred cooking oil. Cook 3 minutes. Brush with reserved marinade. Cook an additional 4 minutes.

4 Divide cooked rice into four serving dishes. Place one salmon fillet in each bowl. Pour remaining reserved marinade on top and serve warm.

Fish Taco Rice Noodle Bowls

The different textures of this recipe, from the crunchy slaw to the delicate, melt-in-your-mouth cod, make this a meal that you'll prepare over and over again!

- **Hands-On Time:** 20 minutes
- **Cook Time:** 20 minutes

Serves 4

For Salsa

1 (8-ounce) can crushed pineapple, drained

1 small shallot, peeled and minced

1 tablespoon chopped fresh cilantro

2 teaspoons lime juice

¼ teaspoon salt

¼ teaspoon ground black pepper

For Slaw

1½ cups grated red cabbage

½ teaspoon granulated sugar

½ teaspoon lime juice

2 tablespoons mayonnaise

1 clove garlic, peeled and minced

¼ teaspoon salt

¼ teaspoon ground black pepper

For Noodle Bowls

8 ounces dry rice noodles, cooked according to package instructions and rinsed

2 teaspoons sesame oil

4 (6-ounce) cod fillets, patted dry

½ teaspoon salt

1 teaspoon Chinese five-spice blend

1. Preheat air fryer at 350°F for 3 minutes.

2. **To make Salsa:** In a small bowl, combine Salsa ingredients. Refrigerate covered until ready to use.

3. **To make Slaw:** In a medium bowl, combine Slaw ingredients. Refrigerate covered until ready to use.

4. **To make Noodle Bowls:** Toss cooked noodles in a medium bowl with sesame oil. While preparing remaining ingredients, continue to toss noodles occasionally to avoid sticking.

5. Place cod fillets on a cutting board and season with salt and Chinese five-spice blend.

6. Place two fillets in air fryer basket lightly greased with preferred cooking oil. Cook 10 minutes until fish is opaque and flakes easily with a fork.

7. Transfer fillets to a large plate and repeat with remaining cod.

8. Distribute noodles among four bowls. Distribute salsa, slaw, and fish evenly among bowls. Serve immediately.

Buffalo-Style Calamari Rings

Calamari can be found in the frozen section of most grocery stores—often already cut into rings. However, fresh squid tubes can be purchased at the fish counter and are easy to slice yourself.

- **Hands-On Time:** 15 minutes
- **Cook Time:** 8 minutes

Serves 4

½ cup buffalo wing sauce

1 cup plain gluten-free bread crumbs

1 teaspoon salt

½ teaspoon ground black pepper

⅓ pound calamari tubes (about 6), cut into ¼"-thick rings

1 lime, quartered

½ cup blue cheese dressing

8 medium celery stalks, cut into thirds

DON'T THROW AWAY THOSE CELERY STALK LEAVES

If your celery has the leaves still attached, don't discard them. Celery leaves are filled with vitamins and minerals. Add while cooking a broth, or chop them up and include in salads, stir-fries, and even your morning green smoothie.

1 Preheat air fryer at 400°F for 3 minutes.

2 Place wing sauce in a small bowl. In a separate shallow dish, combine bread crumbs, salt, and pepper. Dredge a calamari ring in wing sauce. Shake off excess sauce, then roll ring through bread crumb mixture. Repeat with remaining rings.

3 Place half of calamari rings in air fryer basket lightly greased with preferred cooking oil. Cook 2 minutes. Flip calamari. Cook an additional 2 minutes.

4 Transfer calamari rings to a large serving dish and repeat with remaining calamari. Squeeze lime quarters over calamari. Serve warm with blue cheese dressing and cut celery on the side.

8
Vegetarian Dishes

When living a gluten-free lifestyle, coupled with being a vegetarian, your recipe options feel even smaller—not to mention the challenge of ensuring that everything is nutritionally balanced. Luckily, the air fryer is here to help, offering countless possibilities for gluten-free, vegetarian, and nutritional meals you can make in minimal time. Whether you are a full-time vegetarian, or just interested in Meatless Mondays, the air fryer has got you covered.

And the gluten-free and vegetarian dishes in this chapter will definitely hit the spot. With recipes ranging from Veggie Burgers and Crispy Tofu and Sweet Potato Bowls, to Giant Nachos and Mini Mushroom-Onion Eggplant Pizzas, you won't tire of these delicious, satisfying meals.

Veggie Burgers

Whether you are strictly vegetarian, or enjoy a mix of meat and vegetarian dishes, you'll agree that these black bean burgers are just good! The black beans are full of nutrients, and the creamy tree nut cheese not only lends flavor but also acts as a binder for the patties. Serve as is or on a bun with your favorite toppings!

- **Hands-On Time:** 10 minutes
- **Cook Time:** 6 minutes

Serves 4

1 cup canned black beans, drained and rinsed

1 slice gluten-free bread, pinched into pieces

1 large egg white

2 tablespoons finely grated carrots

2 tablespoons finely diced seeded green bell pepper

¼ teaspoon ground cumin

¼ teaspoon smoked paprika

2 tablespoons creamy tree nut cheese

1 tablespoon olive oil

1 Preheat air fryer to 350°F for 3 minutes.

2 In a medium bowl, mash black beans. Add bread pieces, egg white, carrots, bell pepper, cumin, smoked paprika, and tree nut cheese. Form mixture into four patties.

3 Place patties in air fryer basket lightly greased with preferred cooking oil. Cook 3 minutes. Flip. Brush patties with olive oil. Cook an additional 3 minutes.

4 Transfer cooked patties to a large plate and serve warm.

Pizza Tofu Bites

These little bites of tasty protein are perfect for an after-school treat or a snack on the weekend. Marinating the tofu helps it soak up the flavors before air frying. Dipping the bites into a bowl of warmed marinara sauce will bring all the ingredients together.

- **Hands-On Time:** 15 minutes
- **Cook Time:** 20 minutes

Serves 4

For Marinade
⅓ cup vegetable broth
2 tablespoons tomato sauce
1 tablespoon nutritional yeast
1 teaspoon Italian seasoning
1 teaspoon granulated sugar
½ teaspoon fennel seeds
½ teaspoon garlic powder
¼ teaspoon salt
¼ teaspoon ground black pepper
14 ounces firm tofu, cut into ¾" cubes

For Breading
⅔ cup plain gluten-free bread crumbs
2 teaspoons nutritional yeast
1 teaspoon Italian seasoning
½ teaspoon salt

For Dip
1 cup marinara sauce, heated

1 **To make Marinade:** Combine all Marinade ingredients in a gallon-sized plastic bag or large bowl. Toss tofu to coat. Refrigerate 30 minutes, tossing tofu once more after 15 minutes.

2 **To make Breading and Pizza Tofu Bites:** Preheat air fryer to 350°F for 3 minutes.

3 In a shallow dish, combine Breading ingredients.

4 Strain marinade from tofu cubes. Dredge in bread crumb mixture.

5 Place half of tofu in air fryer basket lightly greased with preferred cooking oil. Cook 5 minutes. Flip tofu. Brush with additional cooking oil. Cook an additional 5 minutes.

6 Transfer cooked tofu to a large plate. Repeat with remaining tofu. Serve warm with marinara dip on the side.

Crispy Tofu and Sweet Potato Bowls

The sweetness from the potatoes and the creaminess from the tofu, along with the crisp exteriors of both ingredients, lend so many flavors and textures to these bowls of deliciousness!

- **Hands-On Time:** 15 minutes
- **Cook Time:** 16 minutes

Serves 2

½ small yellow onion, peeled and sliced

1 cup small-diced peeled sweet potato

1 teaspoon avocado oil

8 ounces extra-firm tofu, cut into ¼" cubes

½ teaspoon smoked paprika

½ teaspoon chili powder

¼ teaspoon salt

2 teaspoons lime zest

1 cup cooked quinoa

2 lime wedges

1 Preheat air fryer to 350°F for 3 minutes.

2 In a medium bowl, combine onion, sweet potato, and avocado oil. In another medium bowl, combine tofu, paprika, chili powder, and salt.

3 Place onion mixture into ungreased air fryer basket. Cook 8 minutes. Stir in tofu mixture. Cook an additional 8 minutes.

4 While tofu is cooking, stir lime zest into cooked quinoa, then portion out quinoa into two serving bowls.

5 Evenly distribute cooked tofu mixture over quinoa. Squeeze one lime wedge over each bowl. Serve immediately.

Stuffed Baked Potatoes with Green Goddess Dressing

Baked potatoes are good, stuffed baked potatoes are even better, and stuffed baked potatoes drizzled with this bright, fresh Green Goddess Dressing are the best!

- **Hands-On Time:** 10 minutes
- **Cook Time:** 48 minutes

Serves 2

For Green Goddess Dressing
¼ cup vegan sour cream
½ medium avocado, peeled, pitted, and diced
2 tablespoons plain unsweetened almond milk
2 teaspoons lemon juice
½ teaspoon lemon zest
1 green onion, roughly chopped
2 cloves garlic, peeled and quartered
¼ cup chopped fresh parsley
½ teaspoon salt
¼ teaspoon ground black pepper

For Potatoes
2 teaspoons olive oil
2 large russet potatoes, scrubbed and perforated with a fork
½ teaspoon salt
¼ teaspoon ground black pepper
1 cup steamed broccoli florets
½ cup canned cannellini beans, drained and rinsed

1 **To make Green Goddess Dressing:** Add Green Goddess Dressing ingredients to a food processor bowl. Pulse until smooth. Transfer to a small bowl and refrigerate covered until ready to use.

2 **To make Potatoes:** Preheat air fryer at 400°F for 3 minutes.

3 Rub olive oil over both potatoes. Season with salt and pepper.

4 Place seasoned potatoes in ungreased air fryer basket. Cook 30 minutes. Flip potatoes. Cook an additional 15 minutes.

5 Transfer cooked potatoes to a cutting board to rest 5 minutes until cool enough to handle. Slice each potato lengthwise (about 1" deep without going all the way through). Pinch ends of each potato together to open up each slice.

6 Stuff broccoli and beans into potatoes and place potatoes back into ungreased air fryer basket. Cook 3 minutes.

7 Transfer stuffed potatoes to a large serving plate. Pour Green Goddess Dressing over potatoes and serve warm.

Giant Nachos

These are essentially crispy tostadas, but "Giant Nachos" just sounds more fun!

- **Hands-On Time:** 10 minutes
- **Cook Time:** 10 minutes

Serves 2

2 tablespoons vegan sour cream

½ teaspoon chili powder

½ teaspoon + ⅛ teaspoon salt, divided

2 (6") soft corn tortillas

2 teaspoons avocado oil

½ cup vegetarian refried beans

¼ cup vegan Cheddar cheese shreds

2 tablespoons sliced black olives

½ cup shredded iceberg lettuce

1 large Roma tomato, seeded and diced

2 lime wedges

1. Preheat air fryer to 400°F for 3 minutes.

2. In a small bowl, combine sour cream, chili powder, and ⅛ teaspoon salt. Set aside.

3. Brush tortillas with oil and sprinkle one side with remaining salt.

4. Place one tortilla in ungreased air fryer basket. Cook 3 minutes. Set aside and repeat with second tortilla.

5. Add refried beans and Cheddar cheese shreds to tortillas. Place one tortilla in air fryer basket and cook 2 minutes. Set aside and repeat with second tortilla.

6. Transfer tortillas to two serving plates and top with black olives, lettuce, and tomatoes. Dollop sour cream mixture on each and serve warm with lime wedges on the side for spritzing.

AREN'T ALL REFRIED BEANS VEGETARIAN?

Beans are gluten-free, but not all refried beans are vegetarian. Actually, many refried beans use animal lard in the preparation. Just be sure to check the label before purchasing to ensure that your choice is vegetarian.

Hearty "Sausage" and Potato-Stuffed Bell Peppers

Whether you're a vegan, a vegetarian, or just celebrating Meatless Monday, these stuffed peppers are the perfect meal. And don't knock meatless sausages before you try them: full of flavor and protein, they add another layer of texture and great taste to your meal.

- **Hands-On Time:** 15 minutes
- **Cook Time:** 57 minutes

Serves 4

2 teaspoons olive oil

2 large russet potatoes, scrubbed and perforated with a fork

2 (3-ounce) meatless Italian sausages, smoked, diced into ¼" cubes

2 tablespoons plain unsweetened almond milk

1 teaspoon olive oil

1 tablespoon Italian seasoning

¼ teaspoon salt

¼ teaspoon ground black pepper

¼ cup canned corn kernels, drained

½ cup vegan mozzarella shreds

4 medium green bell peppers, tops and insides discarded

1 Preheat air fryer at 400°F for 3 minutes.

2 Rub olive oil over both potatoes. Place in ungreased air fryer basket and cook 30 minutes. Flip potatoes. Cook an additional 15 minutes.

3 Transfer cooked potatoes to a cutting board and let rest 5 minutes until cool enough to handle. Scoop out cooled potato into a medium bowl. Discard skins.

4 Add sausage to ungreased fryer basket and cook 2 minutes.

5 Using back of a fork, combine potatoes with almond milk, olive oil, Italian seasoning, salt, and black pepper. Toss in cooked Italian sausage, corn, and mozzarella.

6 Stuff peppers with potato mixture. Add peppers to ungreased air fryer basket and cook 10 minutes.

7 Transfer cooked peppers to a large plate and serve warm.

Fried Avocado Tacos

The breaded avocado "fries" are amazingly crisp on the outside and divinely smooth on the inside. And with avocado already found in many Mexican dishes, they're a natural fit for these tacos. Topped with the crunchy slaw, fresh salsa, and a creamy kick from the Sriracha Mayonnaise, these Fried Avocado Tacos will quickly become a household favorite.

- **Hands-On Time: 10 minutes**
- **Cook Time: 10 minutes**

Serves 3

For Salsa

2 medium Roma tomatoes, seeded and diced

¼ cup finely diced peeled red onion

1 tablespoon fresh lime juice

1 teaspoon lime zest

¼ cup chopped fresh cilantro

1 teaspoon salt

For Avocado Fries

Vegan egg substitute equaling 1 large egg

2 tablespoons plain unsweetened almond milk

1 cup plain gluten-free bread crumbs

1 large avocado, peeled, pitted, and sliced into 6 "fries"

For Tacos

6 (6") gluten-free flour tortillas

1 cup coleslaw mix

1 batch Sriracha Mayonnaise (Chapter 3)

1. **To make Salsa:** Combine Salsa ingredients in a small bowl and refrigerate covered until ready to use.

2. **To make Avocado Fries:** Preheat air fryer to 375°F for 3 minutes.

3. Whisk together egg substitute and almond milk in a small bowl. Add bread crumbs to a separate shallow dish.

4. Dip avocado slices in egg mixture. Dredge in bread crumbs.

5. Place half of avocado slices into air fryer basket lightly greased with preferred cooking oil. Cook 5 minutes.

6. Transfer cooked avocado slices to a large serving plate. Repeat with remaining avocado slices.

7. **To make Tacos:** Add two fried avocado fries to each tortilla. Top with coleslaw mix, salsa, and Sriracha Mayonnaise. Serve.

Eggplant Dip

Otherwise known as baba ghanoush, this bold and flavorful Middle Eastern dish is not only tasty, but is also healthy thanks to the nutritious eggplant. The air fryer helps lend a smoky taste to this classic dip.

- **Hands-On Time: 5 minutes**
- **Cook Time: 27 minutes**

Serves 4

2½ teaspoons olive oil, divided

1 medium eggplant, halved lengthwise

2 teaspoons pine nuts

¼ cup tahini

1 tablespoon lemon juice

2 cloves garlic, peeled and minced

⅛ teaspoon ground cumin

¼ teaspoon salt

⅛ teaspoon ground black pepper

1 tablespoon chopped fresh parsley

WHAT TO SERVE WITH EGGPLANT DIP

This dip goes perfectly with slices of gluten-free pita bread or a vegetable assortment of chopped carrots, celery, cauliflower, cucumbers, radishes, and bell peppers.

1 Preheat air fryer at 375°F for 3 minutes.

2 Rub 2 teaspoons oil over both eggplant halves. Pierce eggplant flesh three times per half with a fork.

3 Place eggplant flat side down in ungreased air fryer basket. Cook 25 minutes.

4 Transfer cooked eggplant to a cutting board and let sit 5 minutes until cool enough to handle.

5 While eggplant cools, add pine nuts to ungreased air fryer basket. Cook 2 minutes, shaking every 30 seconds to ensure they don't burn. Set aside in a small bowl.

6 Scoop out eggplant flesh and add to a food processor bowl. Pulse together with tahini, lemon juice, garlic, cumin, salt, and pepper.

7 Transfer dip to a medium bowl. Garnish with roasted pine nuts, chopped parsley, and remaining olive oil.

Mini Mushroom-Onion Eggplant Pizzas

This dish has all of the flavors of a vegetable pizza—without any of the gluten. Serve this recipe alongside a salad of fresh mixed greens for a tummy full of healthy ingredients. If you don't eat dairy, vegan mozzarella shreds can be substituted for the regular mozzarella.

- **Hands-On Time:** 5 minutes
- **Cook Time:** 16 minutes

Serves 4

2 teaspoons + 2 tablespoons olive oil, divided
¼ cup small-diced peeled yellow onion
½ cup small-diced white mushrooms
½ cup marinara sauce
1 small eggplant, sliced into 8 (½") circles
1 teaspoon salt
1 cup shredded mozzarella
¼ cup chopped fresh basil

1 In a medium skillet over medium heat, heat 2 teaspoons olive oil 30 seconds. Add onion and mushrooms and cook 5 minutes until onions are translucent. Add marinara sauce and stir. Remove skillet from heat.

2 Preheat air fryer at 375°F for 3 minutes.

3 Rub remaining olive oil over both sides of eggplant circles. Lay circles on a large plate and season tops evenly with salt. Top with marinara sauce mixture, followed by shredded mozzarella.

4 Place half of eggplant pizzas in ungreased air fryer basket. Cook 5 minutes.

5 Transfer cooked pizzas to a large plate. Repeat with remaining pizzas. Garnish with chopped basil and serve warm.

Marinara Spaghetti Squash

This squash is a favorite because it resembles spaghetti noodles. And you can even spin the "noodles" around on your fork in true Italian fashion!

- **Hands-On Time:** 5 minutes
- **Cook Time:** 25 minutes

Serves 2

2 teaspoons olive oil

½ teaspoon salt

1 (1½-pound) spaghetti squash, halved and seeded

1 cup marinara sauce, heated

2 tablespoons chopped fresh basil leaves

1 Preheat air fryer at 375°F for 3 minutes.

2 Rub olive oil and salt over both halves spaghetti squash. Place squash halves flat side down in ungreased air fryer basket and cook 25 minutes. If you have a wider squash, set halves up along the sides of the basket.

3 Transfer squash to a cutting board and let cool 10 minutes until easy to handle. Using a fork, gently scoop squash "noodles" into a medium bowl. Toss with marinara sauce, garnish with basil leaves, and serve warm.

Breaded Mushrooms

Do you miss sharing those classic breaded mushrooms at restaurants when out with a group of friends? Have you believed up until now that you would have to swear off them forever because of the gluten? Well, invite that group of friends to your house to enjoy a healthier, equally delicious version. Your friends will appreciate your effort *and* these very tasty Breaded Mushrooms!

- **Hands-On Time:** 10 minutes
- **Cook Time:** 7 minutes

Serves 2

2 cups gluten-free crispy rice cereal

1 teaspoon Italian seasoning

1 teaspoon nutritional yeast

⅛ teaspoon salt

1 tablespoon Dijon mustard

1 tablespoon vegan mayonnaise

¼ cup plain unsweetened almond milk

8 ounces whole white mushrooms

1 In a food processor, pulse cereal, Italian seasoning, nutritional yeast, and salt until a bread crumb consistency forms. Transfer to a shallow dish.

2 In a medium bowl, whisk together mustard, mayonnaise, and almond milk.

3 Preheat air fryer to 350°F for 3 minutes.

4 Dip mushrooms in wet mixture. Shake off any excess. Dredge in dry mixture. Shake off any excess.

5 Place mushrooms in air fryer basket lightly greased with preferred cooking oil and cook 4 minutes. Gently shake basket. Cook an additional 3 minutes.

6 Transfer cooked mushrooms to a large plate and serve warm.

Picnic Broccoli Salad

Filled with texture and flavor, this Picnic Broccoli Salad will be the hit side dish of any gathering, no matter what diet you or your companions follow. The air fryer cooks the broccoli perfectly, giving the outside a little crunch.

- **Hands-On Time:** 10 minutes
- **Cook Time:** 5 minutes

Serves 2

1 large bunch broccoli, cut into bite-sized florets

1 tablespoon olive oil

1 tablespoon balsamic vinegar

2 tablespoons water

2 tablespoons raisins

2 tablespoons roasted, salted pepitas

2 tablespoons diced peeled red onion

¼ cup vegan mayonnaise

⅛ teaspoon ground black pepper

1 Preheat air fryer at 350°F for 3 minutes.

2 In a large bowl, combine florets, olive oil, and balsamic vinegar.

3 Pour water into bottom of air fryer. Add florets to ungreased air fryer basket and cook 5 minutes.

4 Transfer florets to a large serving dish. Toss with raisins, pepitas, onion, mayonnaise, and black pepper. Refrigerate covered until ready to serve.

Vegan Caprese Sandwiches

Usually a classic caprese salad is served with a crisp artisan bread so you can sop up the flavors. Now enjoy that delicious salad in sandwich form! Don't overlook the last drizzle of olive oil on the sandwich bread: it pulls all of those traditional flavors together.

- **Hands-On Time:** 10 minutes
- **Cook Time:** 10 minutes

Serves 2

2 tablespoons balsamic vinegar

4 slices gluten-free sandwich bread

2 ounces vegan mozzarella shreds

2 medium Roma tomatoes, sliced

8 fresh basil leaves

2 tablespoons olive oil

1 Preheat air fryer at 350°F for 3 minutes.

2 Prepare sandwiches by drizzling balsamic vinegar on bottom bread slices. Layer mozzarella, tomatoes, and basil leaves on top. Add top bread slices.

3 Brush outside top and bottom of each sandwich lightly with olive oil. Place one sandwich in ungreased air fryer basket and cook 3 minutes. Flip and cook an additional 2 minutes. Transfer sandwich to a large serving plate and repeat with second sandwich.

4 Serve warm.

Cheesy Bean Taquitos

Taquitos are so simple in their ingredients, and the air fryer gives them perfectly crisp exteriors. Vegan cheese has made leaps and bounds from its first introduction to the grocery store shelf, and now you'll discover many options that provide the ooey-gooeyness of regular cheese.

- **Hands-On Time:** 10 minutes
- **Cook Time:** 12 minutes

Yields 15 taquitos

1 cup vegetarian refried beans

2 cups dairy-free Cheddar shreds

15 (6") soft corn tortillas

1 Preheat air fryer at 350°F for 3 minutes.

2 Evenly spread refried beans and Cheddar shreds down center of each corn tortilla. Roll each tortilla tightly and place seam side down on a large serving platter.

3 Place five rolled tortillas, seam side down, in ungreased air fryer basket. Cook 4 minutes.

4 Transfer cooked taquitos back to serving platter and repeat with remaining tortillas. Serve warm.

Chili Quinoa Patties

These Chili Quinoa Patties are a nutritionally balanced meal full of chili flavor! The dairy-free tree nut cheese and cooked quinoa help to bind these patties together, while also lending a rich, earthy taste. Enjoy these as is or on gluten-free hamburger buns with your favorite toppings.

- **Hands-On Time:** 10 minutes
- **Cook Time:** 7 minutes

Serves 4

⅓ cup water

1 tablespoon + ½ teaspoon olive oil, divided

½ teaspoon ground cumin

½ teaspoon garlic salt

⅓ cup uncooked quinoa

1 cup canned tri-bean blend, drained and rinsed

2 tablespoons finely chopped peeled yellow onion

2 tablespoons chopped fresh cilantro

1 teaspoon chili powder

½ teaspoon salt

2 tablespoons creamy tree nut cheese

1 In a small saucepan over high heat, bring water, 1 tablespoon olive oil, cumin, and garlic salt to a boil. Remove from heat and stir in quinoa. Cover and let rest 5 minutes.

2 Preheat air fryer to 350°F for 3 minutes.

3 In a medium bowl, mash beans with back of a fork. Add cooked quinoa, onion, cilantro, chili powder, salt, and tree nut cheese. Combine, then form mixture into four patties.

4 Place patties in air fryer basket lightly greased with preferred cooking oil. Cook 3 minutes. Flip patties. Brush tops with remaining olive oil. Cook an additional 3 minutes.

5 Transfer cooked patties to a large plate and serve warm.

Vegetarian Lasagna

This lasagna contains dairy, so beware if you are a vegan or have issues with lactose. The oven-ready noodles are the key to the ease of this Italian casserole.

- **Hands-On Time:** 15 minutes
- **Cook Time:** 22 minutes

Serves 4

1 medium zucchini, diced

½ cup diced white mushrooms

¼ cup diced peeled yellow onion

1 cup marinara sauce

1 cup ricotta cheese

⅓ cup grated Parmesan cheese

1 large egg

2 teaspoons Italian seasoning

½ teaspoon salt, divided

5 sheets gluten-free oven-ready lasagna noodles

1 cup grated mozzarella cheese

1 In a medium skillet over medium-high heat, cook zucchini, mushrooms, and onion 4 minutes until vegetables are tender.

2 Stir marinara sauce into skillet. Bring to boil over high heat, then reduce heat to medium and simmer 3 minutes.

3 Preheat air fryer at 375°F for 3 minutes.

4 In a small bowl, combine ricotta cheese, Parmesan cheese, egg, Italian seasoning, and salt.

5 Spoon one-fourth of vegetable mixture into an ungreased 7" cake barrel. Place a layer of lasagna noodles on top, breaking apart noodles first to fit pan. Top with one-third ricotta mixture, followed by one-fourth mozzarella. Repeat two more times with vegetables, noodles, ricotta, and mozzarella. Finish with remaining vegetables and mozzarella.

6 Cover lasagna with aluminum foil and place barrel in air fryer basket. Cook 12 minutes. Remove foil and cook uncovered an additional 3 minutes.

7 Remove lasagna from air fryer and let rest 10 minutes. Slice and serve warm.

Two-Ingredient Barbecue Pulled Jackfruit

It just doesn't get any easier than this. Jackfruit pulls apart just like pork, and creates the perfect vehicle for your favorite flavors. Cook with your choice of sauce and serve over rice, on gluten-free buns, or straight out of the bowl.

- **Hands-On Time:** 5 minutes
- **Cook Time:** 10 minutes

Serves 2

1 (20-ounce) can green jackfruit in brine, drained and chopped

⅔ cup barbecue sauce, divided

WHAT IS JACKFRUIT?

Jackfruit is a highly nutritious fruit that can also be found canned. Depending on how ripe it is, it can be used in sweet or savory dishes. When not ripe, it has a neutral flavor that makes it an amazing meat replacement. It takes on any flavor it is paired with, such as the barbecue sauce in this recipe.

1 Preheat air fryer at 375°F for 3 minutes.

2 Toss jackfruit with ⅓ cup barbecue sauce in a medium bowl.

3 Place jackfruit into air fryer basket lightly greased with preferred cooking oil. Cook 5 minutes. Shake basket. Cook an additional 5 minutes.

4 Transfer jackfruit to a medium bowl. Add remaining sauce. Using two forks, pull apart jackfruit to resemble pulled pork. Serve warm.

Shepherdless Pie

Loaded with vegetables and beefless grounds, this Shepherdless Pie delivers all the punch that meat lovers crave. The rich filling is topped with creamy, cheesy mashed potatoes. For a decorative effect, pipe dollops of the mashed potatoes on top of the pie before cooking.

- **Hands-On Time:** 15 minutes
- **Cook Time:** 21 minutes

Serves 4

For Potato Topping

1 large russet potato, peeled and diced

1 tablespoon avocado oil

¼ cup nondairy Cheddar shreds

2 tablespoons plain unsweetened almond milk

½ teaspoon salt

½ teaspoon ground black pepper

For Filling

2 teaspoons avocado oil

1 cup beefless grounds

½ small yellow onion, peeled and diced

1 medium carrot, peeled and diced

¼ cup diced seeded green bell pepper

1 small celery stalk, diced

⅔ cup tomato sauce

1 teaspoon chopped fresh rosemary

1 teaspoon fresh thyme leaves

½ teaspoon salt

½ teaspoon ground black pepper

1 **To make Potato Topping:** Place a large pot of salted water over high heat and bring to a boil. Add diced potatoes and cook approximately 5 minutes until fork tender.

2 Drain potatoes and transfer to a medium bowl. Add avocado oil, Cheddar shreds, almond milk, salt, and pepper. Mash until smooth. Set aside.

3 **To make Filling:** Add avocado oil, beefless grounds, onion, carrot, bell pepper, and celery to a large skillet over medium-high heat. Cook 4 minutes until vegetables are tender. Add tomato sauce, rosemary, thyme, salt, and black pepper. Stir, then remove from heat and set aside.

4 Preheat air fryer at 350°F for 3 minutes.

5 Spoon Filling into a 7" round cake barrel lightly greased with preferred cooking oil. Top with Potato Topping. Using tines of a fork, create shallow lines along top of mashed potatoes.

6 Place cake barrel in ungreased air fryer basket. Cook 12 minutes.

7 Remove barrel from air fryer and let rest 10 minutes. Serve warm.

"Grilled" Pineapple Salsa

The sweetness of the pineapple is enhanced through the heating process. Serve this delicious salsa on salads, with chips, or even atop vegetable burgers. The flavor explosion is worth your time!

- **Hands-On Time:** 5 minutes
- **Cook Time:** 8 minutes

Yields approximately 2 cups

For Pineapple
1 cup (¼") cubes fresh
    pineapple
⅛ teaspoon salt
¼ teaspoon olive oil
Juice of 1 lime wedge

For Salsa
1 large jalapeño, seeded and
    diced
2 medium Roma tomatoes,
    seeded and diced
1 small avocado, peeled,
    pitted, and diced
¼ cup diced peeled red
    onion
1 tablespoon chopped fresh
    cilantro
2 cloves garlic, peeled and
    minced
½ teaspoon granulated sugar
Juice of ½ lime
¼ teaspoon salt

1 **To make Pineapple:** Preheat air fryer at 400°F for 3 minutes.

2 In a small bowl, toss pineapple with salt, olive oil, and lime juice.

3 Place pineapple in air fryer basket lightly greased with preferred cooking oil. Cook 4 minutes. Shake basket. Cook an additional 4 minutes.

4 **To make Salsa:** Transfer pineapple to a medium bowl. Add Salsa ingredients and toss. Refrigerate up to two days until ready to serve.

Leftover Chili Dogs

When you want that grill flavor, but don't have the time, break out your air fryer. Within five minutes you will be on your very own personal picnic.

- **Hands-On Time: 5 minutes**
- **Cook Time: 5 minutes**

Serves 4

4 vegan hot dogs
4 gluten-free hot dog buns
½ cup leftover vegetarian chili, warmed
2 tablespoons Dijon mustard

1 Preheat air fryer to 400°F for 3 minutes.

2 Add hot dogs to ungreased air fryer basket. Cook 4 minutes.

3 Transfer hot dogs to hot dog buns. Place back into air fryer basket. Cook an additional 1 minute.

4 Transfer hot dogs in buns to a large plate and garnish with warmed chili and mustard. Serve warm.

Santa Fe Rice Bowls

These bowls have protein from the black beans and nutrients galore from the many spices and vegetables. Although this recipe calls for brown rice, you can use what is already in your pantry, from different varieties of rice to quinoa.

- **Hands-On Time:** 5 minutes
- **Cook Time:** 5 minutes

Serves 4

1 cup vegan sour cream

2 tablespoons plain unsweetened almond milk

1 teaspoon ground cumin

1 teaspoon chili powder

⅛ teaspoon cayenne pepper

½ teaspoon salt

1 cup canned black beans, drained and rinsed

1 cup canned corn kernels, drained

1 teaspoon olive oil

4 cups cooked brown rice

3 medium Roma tomatoes, diced

1 medium avocado, peeled, pitted, and diced

1 In a medium bowl, combine sour cream, almond milk, cumin, chili powder, cayenne pepper, and salt. Refrigerate covered until ready to use.

2 Preheat air fryer to 350°F for 3 minutes.

3 In a medium bowl, toss beans and corn with olive oil. Place mixture in ungreased air fryer basket and cook 5 minutes.

4 Distribute brown rice among four serving bowls. Top with black bean and corn mixture, tomatoes, and avocado. Drizzle sour cream mixture over top of each bowl and serve immediately.

WANT TO ADD A LITTLE CRUNCH?
Make some crunchy corn strips to add to this dish or even to fresh salads. Slice two corn tortillas into ½" strips. Brush strips with 1 tablespoon olive oil and sprinkle with ⅓ teaspoon salt. Cook strips in ungreased air fryer basket 4 minutes at 400°F, shaking once halfway through cooking. Allow to cool before using.

9

Desserts

When living a gluten-free lifestyle, sweet treats are often a hard food category to navigate because all of the cakes, pies, cobblers, cookies, and more are usually filled with that one pesky ingredient: gluten. Many people assume that gluten-free desserts are less tasty, and also harder to bake at home due to this restriction. But flavor and ease of preparation do not have to be compromised! There are so many great gluten-free flours and other baking ingredients available which will allow you to expand your sweet tooth. And the air fryer will make them a snap to bake!

With recipes ranging from Spice Cake with Orange Cream Cheese Frosting and Margarita Cupcakes, to Pecan Pie Bread Pudding and Mexican Chocolate Custard, the sweet delights in this chapter are guaranteed to hit the spot...no matter what you find yourself craving. See if your family members or party guests can tell the difference (we bet not).

Pretzel-Topped Strawberry Donut Bites

Do you have that one relative who always brings that classic dessert for holiday celebrations? The one with layers of Jell-O, strawberries, and pretzels? These delicious donut bites are a fun and modern twist on that favorite!

- **Hands-On Time:** 10 minutes
- **Cook Time:** 11 minutes

Yields 10 donut bites

For Donut Bites
⅔ cup gluten-free all-purpose flour
⅛ teaspoon salt
½ teaspoon baking powder
1 teaspoon vanilla extract
2 tablespoons light brown sugar
½ cup finely diced hulled fresh strawberries
3 tablespoons whole milk
1 tablespoon butter, melted

For Glaze
2 tablespoons powdered sugar
2 teaspoons whole milk
¼ cup crushed gluten-free pretzels

1 **To make Donut Bites:** In a medium bowl, combine flour, salt, baking powder, vanilla, and brown sugar.

2 Use paper towels to gently squeeze moisture out of strawberries. Add to flour mixture. Add milk and butter. Stir until combined.

3 Preheat air fryer at 325°F for 5 minutes.

4 Form donut mixture into ten (1") balls and place on a pizza pan lightly greased with preferred cooking oil.

5 Place pizza pan in air fryer basket. Cook 11 minutes.

6 Transfer cooked balls to a cooling rack and let cool 5 minutes.

7 **To make Glaze:** In a small bowl, whisk together Glaze ingredients, 1 teaspoon of milk at a time, until desired consistency is reached. Gently pour Glaze over donut balls. Sprinkle with crushed pretzels and serve warm or cold.

Blueberry Orange Biscuit Shortcakes

Who said you could have a shortcake only with strawberries? This blueberry-and-orange combination is here to prove them wrong. You and your loved ones will want second helpings of this delicious, gluten-free twist on the classic dessert.

- **Hands-On Time:** 15 minutes
- **Cook Time:** 16 minutes

Yields 8 shortcakes

For Blueberry Topping
1 pound fresh blueberries, halved
¼ cup granulated sugar
1 teaspoon orange zest

For Whipped Cream
1 cup heavy cream
1 tablespoon fresh orange juice
2 tablespoons powdered sugar

For Biscuits
2 cups gluten-free all-purpose flour
1 tablespoon baking powder
½ teaspoon baking soda
½ teaspoon xanthan gum
½ teaspoon salt
½ teaspoon granulated sugar
4 tablespoons cold butter, cubed
1¼ cups buttermilk

1 **To make Blueberry Topping:** In a small bowl, combine blueberries, sugar, and orange zest. Refrigerate covered until ready to use.

2 **To make Whipped Cream:** In a small metal bowl, beat together heavy cream, orange juice, and powdered sugar 2 minutes until medium peaks form. Refrigerate covered until ready to use.

3 **To make Biscuits:** In a small bowl, combine flour, baking powder, baking soda, xanthan gum, salt, and sugar. Add butter and buttermilk until a sticky dough forms.

4 Preheat air fryer at 350°F for 3 minutes.

5 Flour your hands and form dough into eight balls. Add four balls to a pizza pan lightly greased with preferred cooking oil. Biscuits will be touching.

6 Place pizza pan in air fryer basket. Cook 8 minutes.

7 Transfer biscuits to serving plates. Repeat with remaining dough balls.

8 Cut cooked biscuits in half. Add portioned blueberry mixture to each biscuit bottom. Place tops of biscuits on blueberry mixture and top with whipped cream. Serve.

Spice Cake with Orange Cream Cheese Frosting

Cinnamon, cloves, ginger, and nutmeg come together to warm your spirit through this homey, gluten-free spice cake. The Cream Cheese Frosting with hints of orange provides a fresh yet rich topping for this scrumptious cake.

- **Hands-On Time:** 15 minutes
- **Cook Time:** 35 minutes

Serves 6

For Spice Cake

- 3 large eggs, whites and yolks separated
- 2 tablespoons buttermilk
- 2 tablespoons vegetable oil
- ½ teaspoon vanilla extract
- 2 tablespoons unsweetened applesauce
- ½ cup gluten-free all-purpose flour
- ¼ cup tapioca flour
- ½ teaspoon xanthan gum
- ¼ cup light brown sugar
- ½ teaspoon baking soda
- 1 teaspoon baking powder
- ½ teaspoon ground cinnamon
- ¼ teaspoon ground cloves
- ¼ teaspoon ground ginger
- ¼ teaspoon ground nutmeg
- ⅛ teaspoon salt

For Cream Cheese Frosting

- 6 ounces cream cheese, room temperature
- 1⅓ cups powdered sugar
- ½ teaspoon vanilla extract
- 2 tablespoons butter, room temperature
- 1 tablespoon orange juice

1. **To make Spice Cake:** Place egg whites in a large metal bowl. Beat until stiff peaks form.

2. Preheat air fryer at 350°F for 3 minutes.

3. In a medium bowl, combine egg yolks and remaining wet ingredients.

4. Add wet ingredients to egg whites and gently combine. Fold in dry ingredients.

5. Spoon cake batter into a 7" round cake barrel lightly greased with preferred cooking oil. Cover with aluminum foil.

6. Place cake pan in air fryer basket. Cook 30 minutes. Remove foil. Cook an additional 5 minutes.

7. Transfer cake pan to a cooling rack to cool 10 minutes. Once cooled, flip cake onto a large serving platter.

8. **To make Cream Cheese Frosting:** Cream together Cream Cheese Frosting ingredients in a small bowl. Spread over cake. Slice and serve.

Pecan Pie Bread Pudding

For optimal bread texture, place the bread out on your kitchen counter the night before baking to let it become a little stiff. That is how bread pudding was originally intended, when day-old bread was used in this simple dessert. Serve warm with a little whipped cream or ice cream.

- **Hands-On Time:** 10 minutes
- **Cook Time:** 15 minutes

Serves 4

2 cups (1") cubes gluten-free sandwich bread

½ cup pecan pieces

3 large eggs

¼ cup half-and-half

¼ cup dark corn syrup

1 teaspoon vanilla extract

2 tablespoons dark brown sugar

¼ teaspoon ground cinnamon

¼ teaspoon salt

1 Place bread pieces in an ungreased 7" square cake barrel and spread pecan pieces evenly over top.

2 In a medium bowl, whisk eggs. Stir in remaining ingredients.

3 Pour egg mixture over bread and pecans in cake barrel. Let sit 10 minutes.

4 Preheat air fryer at 325°F for 3 minutes.

5 Place cake pan in air fryer basket. Cook 15 minutes.

6 Transfer pan to a cooling rack for 10 minutes. Once cooled slightly, slice and serve warm.

FRESH VANILLA BEAN SUBSTITUTION

Although vanilla extract is easily accessible and relatively inexpensive, vanilla beans are just the bee's knees when fresh taste is at stake. Simply substitute a 2" portion of a vanilla bean for 1 teaspoon of vanilla extract. Scrape out the seeds and add them to your recipe!

Pumpkin Crunch Cake

It may seem like this cake has a lot of ingredients you'll need to run to the store for, but look closely: you should have most of them already in your home! This is a beautifully moist cake with a crunch layer similar to a cheesecake crust. Everything is brought together by the sinful Cream Cheese Frosting. To. Die. For.

- **Hands-On Time:** 15 minutes
- **Cook Time:** 35 minutes

Serves 6

For Crunch Layer
⅓ cup pecan pieces
5 gluten-free gingersnap cookies
⅓ cup light brown sugar
3 tablespoons butter, melted

For Cake
3 large eggs
3 tablespoons butter, melted
½ teaspoon vanilla extract
1 cup pumpkin purée
2 tablespoons sour cream
½ cup gluten-free all-purpose flour
¼ cup tapioca flour
½ teaspoon xanthan gum
½ cup granulated sugar
½ teaspoon baking soda
1 teaspoon baking powder
1 teaspoon pumpkin pie spice
⅛ teaspoon salt

For Cream Cheese Frosting
6 ounces cream cheese, room temperature
1⅓ cups powdered sugar
½ teaspoon vanilla extract
2 tablespoons butter, room temperature
1 tablespoon whole milk

1. Cut a piece of parchment paper to fit inside bottom of a 7" round cake barrel. Place parchment paper in pan. Brush paper and sides of pan lightly with preferred cooking oil.

2. **To make Crunch Layer:** In a food processor, pulse Crunch Layer ingredients until combined. Press mixture into bottom of cake pan.

3. **To make Cake:** Whisk together wet cake ingredients in a medium bowl. In a large bowl, sift together dry cake ingredients.

4. Preheat air fryer at 350°F for 3 minutes.

5. Add wet ingredients to dry ingredients and gently combine. Do not overmix. Pour mixture into cake pan. Cover with aluminum foil.

6. Place cake pan in air fryer basket. Cook 30 minutes. Remove foil. Cook an additional 5 minutes.

7. Transfer cake pan to a cooling rack to cool 10 minutes. Once cooled, flip cake onto a large serving platter.

8. **To make Cream Cheese Frosting:** Cream together frosting ingredients in a small bowl. Spread over cooled cake. Slice and serve.

Strawberry Cupcakes

By adding the strawberries to both the cake and the buttercream frosting, you get double the strawberry flavor. And, if you really like to see a pink color in your cupcakes, squirt a few drops of food coloring into the cupcake batter!

- **Hands-On Time:** 10 minutes
- **Cook Time:** 14 minutes

Yields 8 cupcakes

For Cupcakes
1 cup gluten-free all-purpose flour
½ teaspoon baking soda
⅓ cup granulated sugar
¼ teaspoon salt
2 tablespoons unsweetened applesauce
1 teaspoon vanilla extract
1 large egg
1 tablespoon butter, melted
¼ cup diced hulled fresh strawberries

For Strawberry Buttercream Frosting
¼ cup diced hulled fresh strawberries
6 tablespoons butter, room temperature
1½ cups powdered sugar
⅛ teaspoon vanilla extract
⅛ teaspoon salt

1. **To make Cupcakes:** In a large bowl, combine flour, baking soda, sugar, and salt. In a medium bowl, combine applesauce, vanilla, egg, and butter.

2. Preheat air fryer at 375°F for 3 minutes.

3. Pour wet ingredients from medium bowl into large bowl with dry ingredients. Gently combine. Fold in strawberries. Spoon mixture into eight silicone cupcake liners lightly greased with preferred cooking oil.

4. Place four cupcake liners into air fryer basket. Cook 7 minutes.

5. Transfer cupcake liners to a cooling rack and let sit 10 minutes. Repeat with remaining cupcakes.

6. **To make Strawberry Buttercream Frosting:** Place strawberries in a food processor and pulse until smooth.

7. Add butter to a small mixing bowl and beat until smooth. Slowly add sugar to butter while beating. Add vanilla, salt, and puréed strawberries. Blend.

8. Spread frosting on cooled cupcakes. Serve.

Carrot Cake Cupcakes

The carrot cake is so rich with spices and flavors and pairs perfectly with the creaminess of the frosting and the earthiness and crunch of the walnuts.

- **Hands-On Time:** 10 minutes
- **Cook Time:** 14 minutes

Yields 8 cupcakes

For Cupcakes
1 cup gluten-free all-purpose flour
½ teaspoon baking soda
⅓ cup light brown sugar
¼ teaspoon salt
¼ teaspoon ground cinnamon
⅛ teaspoon ground ginger
1 teaspoon vanilla extract
1 large egg
1 tablespoon buttermilk
1 tablespoon vegetable oil
¼ cup grated carrots
2 tablespoons coconut shreds

For Cream Cheese Frosting
6 ounces cream cheese, room temperature
1⅓ cups powdered sugar
½ teaspoon vanilla extract
2 tablespoons butter, room temperature
1 tablespoon whole milk
½ cup chopped walnuts

1 **To make Cupcakes:** In a large bowl, combine flour, baking soda, sugar, salt, cinnamon, ginger, and vanilla. In a medium bowl, combine egg, buttermilk, oil, carrots, and coconut.

2 Preheat air fryer at 375°F for 3 minutes.

3 Pour wet ingredients from medium bowl into large bowl with dry ingredients. Gently combine. Do not overmix. Spoon mixture into eight silicone cupcake liners lightly greased with preferred cooking oil.

4 Place four cupcake liners in air fryer basket. Cook 7 minutes.

5 Transfer cooked cupcakes to a cooling rack and let sit for 15 minutes. Repeat with remaining cupcakes.

6 **To make Cream Cheese Frosting:** In a small bowl, beat cream cheese, sugar, vanilla, butter, and milk until smooth.

7 Spread frosting on cooled cupcakes. Sprinkle tops with chopped walnuts. Serve.

Margarita Cupcakes

These cupcakes are a perfectly moist, delectable blend of the flavors of tequila, orange, and lime—all present in the classic margarita. And, don't forget to add a pinch of coarse salt to the finished products to mimic that salted rim.

- **Hands-On Time:** 10 minutes
- **Cook Time:** 14 minutes

Yields 8 cupcakes

For Cupcakes
1 cup gluten-free all-purpose flour
½ teaspoon baking soda
⅓ cup granulated sugar
¼ teaspoon salt
2 tablespoons tequila, divided
1 tablespoon orange juice
1 tablespoon lime juice
2 teaspoons lime zest
1 teaspoon vanilla extract
1 large egg
1 tablespoon butter, melted

For Citrus Buttercream Frosting
6 tablespoons butter, room temperature
1½ cups powdered sugar
1 tablespoon tequila
1 teaspoon orange juice
1 teaspoon lime juice
⅛ teaspoon salt
1 teaspoon coarse salt

1 **To make Cupcakes:** In a large bowl, combine flour, baking soda, sugar, and salt. In a medium bowl, combine 1 tablespoon tequila, orange juice, lime juice, lime zest, vanilla, egg, and butter.

2 Preheat air fryer at 375°F for 3 minutes.

3 Pour wet ingredients from medium bowl into large bowl with dry ingredients. Gently combine. Do not overmix. Spoon mixture into eight silicone cupcake liners lightly greased with preferred cooking oil.

4 Place four cupcake liners in air fryer basket. Cook 7 minutes.

5 Transfer cooked cupcakes to a cooling rack and let sit for 15 minutes. Repeat with remaining cupcakes.

6 Brush remaining tablespoon of tequila over cooled cupcakes.

7 **To make Citrus Buttercream Frosting:** Add butter to a medium mixing bowl and beat until smooth. Slowly add sugar while still beating. Add tequila, orange juice, lime juice, and ⅛ teaspoon salt.

8 Spread frosting on cooled cupcakes. Sprinkle salt on top. Serve.

Apple Crumble Jars

These tasty little individual desserts taste even better with a dollop of fresh whipped cream or a scoop of vanilla ice cream. Make ahead for picnics or after-school treats, or whip up after a day of apple picking with the family!

- **Hands-On Time:** 15 minutes
- **Cook Time:** 24 minutes

Serves 6

For Apple Filling

3 cups diced, peeled, seeded Granny Smith apples (approximately 3 large)

1 tablespoon lemon juice

1 tablespoon gluten-free all-purpose flour

2 tablespoons light brown sugar

½ teaspoon ground cinnamon

1 tablespoon butter, melted

⅛ teaspoon salt

6 (4-ounce) glass jelly jars

For Crumble Topping

2 tablespoons gluten-free all-purpose flour

⅓ cup old-fashioned oats

¼ cup chopped pecans

4 teaspoons light brown sugar

¼ teaspoon ground cinnamon

⅛ teaspoon ground nutmeg

2 tablespoons butter, melted

⅛ teaspoon salt

1 **To make Apple Filling:** Place diced apples in a medium bowl and toss with lemon juice. Add remaining filling ingredients and toss.

2 Preheat air fryer at 350°F for 3 minutes.

3 Distribute apple mixture among jelly jars. Place three jars in air fryer basket. Cook 7 minutes. Repeat with remaining jars.

4 **To make Crumble Topping:** While apple mixture is cooking, combine Crumble Topping ingredients in a medium bowl.

5 Spoon Crumble Topping over cooked apples. Bake an additional 5 minutes in batches of three jars.

6 Let jars cool 10 minutes before covering. Refrigerate until ready to serve, up to 4 days.

Ginger Pear Crumble Jars

For an extra-decadent dessert, whip up some fresh cream and add a pinch or two of cinnamon. You can also serve with scoops of vanilla ice cream and let the flavors from the recipe shine through!

- **Hands-On Time:** 15 minutes
- **Cook Time:** 24 minutes

Serves 6

For Pear Filling

3 cups diced, peeled, seeded pears (approximately 4 large)

1 tablespoon lemon juice

1 tablespoon gluten-free all-purpose flour

2 tablespoons dark brown sugar

½ teaspoon ground ginger

1 tablespoon butter, melted

⅛ teaspoon salt

6 (4-ounce) glass jelly jars

For Crumble Topping

2 tablespoons gluten-free all-purpose flour

6 gluten-free gingersnap cookies

¼ cup chopped pecans

4 teaspoons light brown sugar

⅛ teaspoon ground nutmeg

2 tablespoons butter, melted

⅛ teaspoon salt

1 **To make Pear Filling:** Place pears in a medium bowl and toss with lemon juice. Add remaining filling ingredients and toss.

2 Preheat air fryer at 350°F for 3 minutes.

3 Distribute pear mixture among jelly jars.

4 Place three jars in air fryer basket. Cook 7 minutes. Set aside and repeat with remaining jars.

5 **To make Crumble Topping:** While jars are cooking, pulse Crumble Topping ingredients together in a food processor until crumbly and a little chunky.

6 Spoon topping over cooked pear mixture. Place three jars back in air fryer and bake an additional 5 minutes. Repeat with remaining jars.

7 Let jars cool 15 minutes before covering. Refrigerate until ready to serve, up to four days.

Magic Bars

Abracadabra! Filled with everything but the kitchen sink, these Magic Bars are a surefire way to turn any frown upside down.

- **Hands-On Time:** 10 minutes
- **Cook Time:** 20 minutes

Yields 6 bars

1½ cups gluten-free crispy rice cereal
¼ cup chopped pecans
½ cup light corn syrup
¼ cup light brown sugar
⅓ cup creamy peanut butter
2 tablespoons chocolate toffee chips
2 tablespoons semi-sweet chocolate chips
2 tablespoons butter, melted
½ teaspoon vanilla extract
⅛ teaspoon salt

1. Combine all ingredients in a medium bowl.
2. Preheat air fryer at 350°F for 3 minutes.
3. Press bar mixture into a 7" square cake barrel lightly greased with preferred cooking oil. Cover with aluminum foil.
4. Place pan in air fryer basket and cook 15 minutes. Remove foil and cook an additional 5 minutes.
5. Remove pan from air fryer and let cool completely, approximately 15 minutes, to allow to set. Once cooled, flip over on a plate and slice into six bars.

Giant Nutty Chocolate Chip Cookies

Pour a tall glass of milk. You are going to need it with these giant cookies filled with nuts and chocolate chips. Change the type of nuts or chips for different cookies every time!

- **Hands-On Time:** 10 minutes
- **Cook Time:** 20 minutes

Serves 2

½ cup gluten-free all-purpose flour
⅛ teaspoon baking soda
¼ cup butter, melted
¼ cup light brown sugar
2 tablespoons granulated sugar
2 large eggs
¼ cup semi-sweet chocolate chips
¼ cup chopped pecans
½ teaspoon vanilla extract
⅛ teaspoon salt

1 Preheat air fryer at 350°F for 3 minutes.

2 Combine all ingredients in a medium bowl.

3 Press half of cookie mixture onto a pizza pan lightly greased with preferred cooking oil.

4 Place pan in air fryer basket and cook 10 minutes.

5 Remove pan from air fryer and let cool completely, about 10 minutes, to allow to set. Once cooled, flip over on a plate and repeat with remaining dough. Serve.

CHIPS, CHIPS, AND MORE CHIPS
These exceptionally yummy cookies call for semi-sweet chocolate chips; however, don't be afraid to mix things up. With options like butterscotch, dark chocolate, white chocolate, peanut butter, and seasonal delights available, these cookies can be different every single time you make them!

Mexican Chocolate Custard

Mexican chocolate is full of spices and is a bit more granular than typical American chocolate. By adding some cinnamon and a touch of almond extract, this custard gets a stamp in its passport south of the border!

- **Hands-On Time: 15 minutes**
- **Cook Time: 24 minutes**

Serves 4

4 large egg yolks

2 tablespoons granulated sugar

⅛ teaspoon salt

⅛ teaspoon almond extract

1½ cups half-and-half

¾ cup semi-sweet chocolate chips

1 teaspoon ground cinnamon

1 In a small bowl, whisk together egg yolks, sugar, salt, and almond extract. Set aside.

2 In a medium saucepan over medium-low heat, bring half-and-half to a low simmer. Whisk a spoonful of heated half-and-half into egg mixture, then slowly whisk egg mixture into saucepan. Add chocolate chips and cinnamon and continually stir 10 minutes until chocolate is melted.

3 Preheat air fryer at 350°F for 3 minutes.

4 Remove pan from heat and evenly distribute chocolate mixture among four ungreased ramekins.

5 Place two ramekins in air fryer basket. Cook 7 minutes.

6 Transfer cooked custards to a cooling rack. Repeat with remaining custards.

7 Allow custards to cool about 15 minutes, then cover and refrigerate at least two hours before serving, up to two days.

Kiwi Pavlova with Lemon Cream

If you've never had pavlova, make this recipe right now. Noted for its crispy exterior and marshmallow-y interior, this beautiful meringue-like dessert was named after Russian ballerina Anna Pavlova. Topped with cream and fresh fruit, this lovely dessert is sure to please.

- **Hands-On Time:** 15 minutes
- **Cook Time:** 90 minutes

Serves 2

For Pavlova
2 egg whites
¼ teaspoon cornstarch
½ cup granulated sugar
½ teaspoon lemon juice
½ teaspoon vanilla extract

For Topping
⅓ cup heavy whipping cream
1 teaspoon lemon juice
¼ teaspoon lemon zest
2 tablespoons granulated sugar
2 medium kiwis, peeled and sliced

1 **To make Pavlova:** Cut a piece of parchment to size of grill pan. Draw a 6" circle on paper. Flip paper, ink side down, onto grill pan. You should be able to see circle outline through paper. Set aside.

2 In a large metal bowl, set an electric mixer to high speed and beat egg whites. Still beating, add cornstarch. Add sugar, 1 tablespoon at a time, until stiff peaks form in mixture. Add lemon juice and vanilla.

3 Preheat air fryer at 225°F for 5 minutes.

4 Spoon or pipe egg white mixture over parchment paper circle, creating higher edges around perimeter (like a short pie crust). There should be an indention in center.

5 Add grill pan to air fryer basket and cook 60 minutes.

6 Once done, turn off heat and leave grill pan with pavlova in air fryer an additional 30 minutes.

7 Remove grill pan from air fryer and gently peel off parchment paper from bottom of pavlova. Transfer pavlova to a large plate.

8 **To make Topping:** In a medium bowl, whisk together whipping cream, lemon juice, lemon zest, and sugar until creamy. Fill pavlova "crust" with whipped cream mixture and top with kiwi slices. Serve.

Chocolate Raspberry Pavlova

The light cream and fresh raspberries are the perfect complements to the chocolatey interior and crispy exterior of the pavlova. Take a few extra minutes to specifically place the raspberry garnishes for a dramatic presentation.

- **Hands-On Time:** 15 minutes
- **Cook Time:** 90 minutes

Serves 2

For Pavlova
2 large egg whites
¼ teaspoon cornstarch
½ cup granulated sugar
1 tablespoon unsweetened cocoa powder
½ teaspoon apple cider vinegar
½ teaspoon vanilla extract

For Topping
⅓ cup heavy whipping cream
2 tablespoons granulated sugar
½ cup fresh raspberries
1 ounce dark chocolate, shaved

1 **To make Pavlova:** Cut a piece of parchment to size of grill pan. Draw a 6″ circle on paper. Flip paper, ink side down, onto grill pan. You should be able to see circle outline through paper. Set aside.

2 In a large metal bowl, set an electric mixer to high speed and beat egg whites. Still beating, add cornstarch. Add sugar, 1 tablespoon at a time, until stiff peaks form in mixture. Gently fold in cocoa powder, apple cider vinegar, and vanilla.

3 Preheat air fryer at 225°F for 5 minutes.

4 Spoon or pipe egg white mixture over parchment paper circle, creating higher edges around perimeter (like a short pie crust). There should be an indention in center.

5 Add grill pan to air fryer basket and cook 60 minutes.

6 Once done, turn off heat and leave grill pan with pavlova in air fryer an additional 30 minutes.

7 Remove grill pan from air fryer and gently peel off parchment paper from bottom of pavlova. Transfer pavlova to a large plate.

8 **To make Topping:** In a medium bowl, whisk together whipping cream and sugar. Fill pavlova "crust" with whipped cream mixture. Garnish with raspberries. Sprinkle shaved chocolate over raspberries and serve.

Amaretto Cheesecake

Change up this delicious recipe by exchanging the Amaretto for Chambord (raspberry) or Grand Marnier (orange).

- **Hands-On Time:** 10 minutes
- **Cook Time:** 22 minutes

Serves 6

For Crust
½ cup Corn Chex
⅔ cup blanched slivered almonds
1 tablespoon light brown sugar
3 tablespoons butter, melted

For Cheesecake
14 ounces cream cheese, room temperature
2 tablespoons sour cream
1 large egg
½ cup granulated sugar
½ cup Amaretto liqueur
½ teaspoon lemon juice
⅛ teaspoon salt

1 **To make Crust:** Pulse Corn Chex, almonds, and brown sugar in a food processor until it has a powdered consistency. Pour into a small bowl and add melted butter. Combine with a fork until butter is well distributed. Press mixture into a 7" springform pan lightly greased with preferred cooking oil.

2 Preheat air fryer at 400°F for 3 minutes.

3 **To make Cheesecake:** Combine cream cheese, sour cream, egg, sugar, Amaretto, lemon juice, and salt in a large bowl. Spoon over crust. Cover with aluminum foil.

4 Place springform pan in air fryer basket and cook 16 minutes. Remove aluminum foil and cook an additional 6 minutes.

5 Remove cheesecake from air fryer basket. Cheesecake will be a little jiggly in center. Cover and refrigerate at least 2 hours to allow it to set. Once set, release side pan and serve.

Chocolate Peanut Butter Cheesecake

Everyone knows that peanut butter and chocolate are a seamless union. So, what could make this couple even better? Adding it to a cheesecake!

- **Hands-On Time:** 10 minutes
- **Cook Time:** 24 minutes

Serves 6

For Crust
1 cup quick-cooking steel-cut oats
1 tablespoon peanut butter powder
1 tablespoon granulated sugar
3 tablespoons butter, melted

For Cheesecake
12 ounces cream cheese, room temperature
2 tablespoons sour cream
2 large eggs
¼ cup unsweetened cocoa powder
½ cup light brown sugar
1 teaspoon vanilla extract
⅛ teaspoon salt
⅔ cup peanut butter chips

1 **To make Crust:** Pulse oats and peanut butter powder in a food processor until they have a powdered consistency. Pour into a small bowl and add sugar and melted butter. Combine with a fork until butter is well distributed. Press mixture into a 7" springform pan lightly greased with preferred cooking oil.

2 Preheat air fryer at 400°F for 3 minutes.

3 **To make Cheesecake:** Combine cream cheese, sour cream, eggs, cocoa, brown sugar, vanilla, and salt in a large bowl. Spoon over crust. Cover with aluminum foil.

4 Place springform pan in air fryer basket and cook 18 minutes. Remove aluminum foil and cook an additional 6 minutes.

5 Remove cheesecake from air fryer. Cheesecake will be a little jiggly in center. Sprinkle with peanut butter chips, cover, and refrigerate at least 2 hours to allow it to set. Once set, release side pan and serve.

WHAT IS PEANUT BUTTER POWDER?
Peanut butter powder is made from pressed-down peanuts that are ground into a powder. Due to the reduced amount of oil, peanut butter powder is lower in calories and fat and higher in protein and fiber than a serving of regular peanuts or peanut butter.

Lemon Cheesecake with Raspberry Sauce

For a grown-up kick to this elegant dessert, add a tablespoon of Chambord to your raspberry sauce and then serve a little on the side for a perfect after-dinner pairing!

- **Hands-On Time:** 10 minutes
- **Cook Time:** 22 minutes

Serves 6

For Crust
1 cup cornflakes cereal
2 tablespoons granulated sugar
4 tablespoons butter, melted

For Cheesecake
12 ounces cream cheese, room temperature
2 tablespoons sour cream
2 large eggs
½ cup granulated sugar
1 tablespoon lemon zest
1 tablespoon fresh lemon juice
1 teaspoon vanilla extract
⅛ teaspoon salt

For Raspberry Sauce
1½ cups fresh raspberries
2 tablespoons lemon juice
½ cup granulated sugar

1 **To make Crust:** Pulse together cornflakes, sugar, and butter in a food processor. Press mixture into a 7" springform pan lightly greased with preferred cooking oil.

2 Preheat air fryer at 400°F for 3 minutes.

3 **To make Cheesecake:** Combine cream cheese, sour cream, eggs, sugar, lemon zest, lemon juice, vanilla, and salt in a large bowl. Spoon into crust. Cover with aluminum foil.

4 Place springform pan in air fryer basket and cook 16 minutes. Remove aluminum foil and cook an additional 6 minutes.

5 **To make Raspberry Sauce:** While cheesecake is baking, add Raspberry Sauce ingredients to a small saucepan over medium heat and cook 5 minutes. Using back of spoon, smoosh raspberries against side of saucepan while cooking. After berries are smooshed and sauce has thickened, pour through a sieve to filter out seeds. Refrigerate covered until ready to use.

6 Remove cheesecake from air fryer. Cheesecake will be a little jiggly in center. Cover and refrigerate at least 2 hours to allow it to set. Once set, release side pan and serve with Raspberry Sauce poured over slices.

Tortilla Sopapillas

Sopapillas have many variations depending on the region; however, they are tradition-ally made out of a pastry wheat dough. But why should folks who are sensitive to gluten be deprived of this very simple yet extremely tasty treat? The gluten-free tortillas in this recipe act as a liaison between tradition and modern. Yum!

- **Hands-On Time:** 5 minutes
- **Cook Time:** 4 minutes

Serves 8

2 tablespoons granulated sugar

½ teaspoon ground cinnamon

⅛ teaspoon salt

8 (6") gluten-free flour tortillas, quartered

2 tablespoons butter, melted

4 teaspoons honey

1 tablespoon powdered sugar

1 Preheat air fryer to 400°F for 5 minutes.

2 In a small bowl, combine sugar, cinnamon, and salt. Set aside.

3 Brush tortilla quarters with melted butter. Sprinkle sugar mixture over brushed tortillas.

4 Add prepared tortillas to ungreased air fryer basket. Cook 2 minutes. Toss tortillas, then cook an additional 2 minutes.

5 Transfer sopapillas to a large plate. Let cool 5 minutes to allow to harden.

6 Drizzle hardened sopapillas with honey and sprinkle with powdered sugar. Serve.

Double Chocolate Nutty Brownies

What is better than chocolate? Double chocolate! The crunch of the pecans is a natural addition to these mouth-watering Double Chocolate Nutty Brownies, although crushed almonds or walnuts work just as well!

- **Hands-On Time:** 10 minutes
- **Cook Time:** 12 minutes

Yields 9 brownies

½ cup gluten-free all-purpose flour

2 tablespoons unsweetened cocoa

⅓ cup granulated sugar

¼ teaspoon baking soda

3 tablespoons unsalted butter, melted

1 large egg

⅛ teaspoon salt

½ cup semi-sweet chocolate chips

¼ cup chopped pecans

1 tablespoon powdered sugar

1 In a medium bowl, combine flour, cocoa, sugar, baking soda, and butter. Stir in egg and salt. Add chocolate chips and chopped pecans, stirring to combine.

2 Preheat air fryer at 350°F for 3 minutes.

3 Press brownie mixture into a 7″ square cake barrel lightly greased with preferred cooking oil.

4 Place cake barrel in air fryer basket. Cook 12 minutes.

5 Remove cake barrel from air fryer and let cool 10 minutes. Slice into nine brownies and garnish with powdered sugar.

US/Metric Conversion Chart

VOLUME CONVERSIONS

US Volume Measure	Metric Equivalent
⅛ teaspoon	0.5 milliliter
¼ teaspoon	1 milliliter
½ teaspoon	2 milliliters
1 teaspoon	5 milliliters
½ tablespoon	7 milliliters
1 tablespoon (3 teaspoons)	15 milliliters
2 tablespoons (1 fluid ounce)	30 milliliters
¼ cup (4 tablespoons)	60 milliliters
⅓ cup	90 milliliters
½ cup (4 fluid ounces)	125 milliliters
⅔ cup	160 milliliters
¾ cup (6 fluid ounces)	180 milliliters
1 cup (16 tablespoons)	250 milliliters
1 pint (2 cups)	500 milliliters
1 quart (4 cups)	1 liter (about)

WEIGHT CONVERSIONS

US Weight Measure	Metric Equivalent
½ ounce	15 grams
1 ounce	30 grams
2 ounces	60 grams
3 ounces	85 grams
¼ pound (4 ounces)	115 grams
½ pound (8 ounces)	225 grams
¾ pound (12 ounces)	340 grams
1 pound (16 ounces)	454 grams

OVEN TEMPERATURE CONVERSIONS

Degrees Fahrenheit	Degrees Celsius
200 degrees F	95 degrees C
250 degrees F	120 degrees C
275 degrees F	135 degrees C
300 degrees F	150 degrees C
325 degrees F	160 degrees C
350 degrees F	180 degrees C
375 degrees F	190 degrees C
400 degrees F	205 degrees C
425 degrees F	220 degrees C
450 degrees F	230 degrees C

BAKING PAN SIZES

American	Metric
8 x 1½ inch round baking pan	20 x 4 cm cake tin
9 x 1½ inch round baking pan	23 x 3.5 cm cake tin
11 x 7 x 1½ inch baking pan	28 x 18 x 4 cm baking tin
13 x 9 x 2 inch baking pan	30 x 20 x 5 cm baking tin
2 quart rectangular baking dish	30 x 20 x 3 cm baking tin
15 x 10 x 2 inch baking pan	30 x 25 x 2 cm baking tin (Swiss roll tin)
9 inch pie plate	22 x 4 or 23 x 4 cm pie plate
7 or 8 inch springform pan	18 or 20 cm springform or loose bottom cake tin
9 x 5 x 3 inch loaf pan	23 x 13 x 7 cm or 2 lb narrow loaf or pâté tin
1½ quart casserole	1.5 liter casserole
2 quart casserole	2 liter casserole

Index

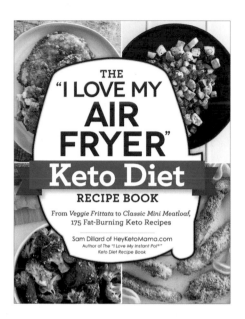